Patiently Waiting on God, While Checking My Watch

By Rachel Williams, PhD

Patiently Waiting on God, While Checking My Watch

Trilogy Christian Publishers A Wholly Owned Subsidiary of Trinity Broadcasting Network

2442 Michelle Drive Tustin, CA 92780

Copyright © 2021 by Rachel Williams

Rights Department, 2442 Michelle Drive, Tustin, CA 92780.

Trilogy Christian Publishing/TBN and colophon are trademarks of Trinity Broadcasting Network.

Cover design by: Grant Swank

For information about special discounts for bulk purchases, please contact Trilogy Christian Publishing.

Trilogy Disclaimer: The views and content expressed in this book are those of the author and may not necessarily reflect the views and doctrine of Trilogy Christian Publishing or the Trinity Broadcasting Network.

Manufactured in the United States of America

10 9 8 7 6 5 4 3 2 1

Library of Congress Cataloging-in-Publication Data is available.

ISBN: 978-1-63769-288-2

E-ISBN: 978-1-63769-289-9

Acknowledgments

To my faithful friends and adopted family: Monica Armstrong, Amy Chambers, Adam Gergen, Dan & Jessica Gillan, Smokey & Melissa Hebert, Mike & ML Henshaw, Jamie & Annie Herring, Olivia Berg & Jon Krog, Peggy Mathews, Roger & Theresa Mathieu, Bob & Michelle VanGerven, dear friends and coaches not listed by name, and my work colleagues who have become adopted family—thank you for your love and friendship along this journey and helping me stay focused on fighting the good fight and finishing the race. Thank you for praying for me so faithfully and for helping pick me up and dust me off on the days the race seemed to get the best of me. Your "Free Therapy" sessions have meant the world to me (and saved me a ton of money). May God bless you as abundantly as you have blessed me.

To Ginny Lee: what a road we have faithfully journeyed together, my precious friend. Day in and day out. One step at a time. Always believing that miracles do happen. Your faith and deep resounding love for the Lord is infectious and has been a model for me to live by.

To my amazing family: Dad & Mom, Stephen & Bethany, Ryan & Michelle, and the little humans Christian, Brooks, and Ava...there are simply no words—none—that can begin to describe what you mean to me. You have been my collective rock through all the good times and all the bad, through all the joys and pain, through all the laughter (much of which you caused) and the tears. Thank you for all the ways you have blessed me, as they are too many to count. I pray that my life is just a fraction of the blessing to you that your lives have been to me. And there is no doubt in my mind, this book would never have seen the light of day without your wise and insightful feedback and persistent encouragement.

To Sam: you were worth every second, every minute, every hour, every day, every week, every month, and the many years of waiting.

God blessed me more than I could have ever imagined when He brought you into my life. Thank you for making me laugh every day, for challenging me intellectually, for helping me grow spiritually, for participating in all my athletic exploits, and for loving me endlessly. You are my best friend and the love of my life. I love you and cannot wait to embark on the adventures God has planned for us.

To my Heavenly Father: You have given me the ability, the vision, and the passion to see this undertaking through to completion. The perseverance you have developed in me over the years has once again helped me accomplish what I believed to be impossible. My life is in Your hands as you continue to guide me in accomplishing the impossible with each day I am given. All for Your glory.

Table of Contents

Introduction

I have recently been through what is undoubtedly the most difficult time of life: a period of waiting. It may sound odd, but those other precious souls who have walked this same road understand that waiting can be one of the most arduous things one has to endure. It is undoubtedly the most trying of the spiritual disciplines. And the difficulty is compounded when God has made you a promise but then requires you to wait for the fulfillment of that promise.

We will all have waiting periods during our lives. Those waiting periods may be as simple as waiting for our order to come up at our favorite restaurant, waiting in the line at the grocery store, or waiting for our coffee to brew at home. Those waiting periods may be as challenging as waiting for test results from our doctor's office, waiting for the right man or woman to come into our lives, or waiting for the Lord to bless us with children. The bottom line is we will all have waiting periods.

I have personally waited far more than I ever hoped to, wanted to, or thought was realistic of my very "get-to-it" personality. Sometimes I waited well, and I sensed the Lord was pleased with my spiritual maturity. Other times I didn't wait so well, looking more like my friend's two-year-old throwing a temper tantrum than the adult woman I am because the Lord was not abiding by my timetable. On those occasions, I have a feeling the Lord looked down at me and shook His head, knowing there was a lot more work to be done on this feeble vessel!

In my periods of waiting well, or at least with the proper attitude, I researched the concept of waiting and did my best to learn everything I could about it. Some of the key questions I asked included the following: what is it? Why does God make us wait? What does waiting require of us? What are the consequences of not waiting? How should we wait? And what are God's promises if we are willing to wait on Him?

I researched "waiting," "waiting on God," "waiting faithfully," "waiting well," "God's promises," and the list goes on. As I collected page after page of information, the Lord began to give me "waiting examples" that I knew I was supposed to capture. So I did, and then one day, I felt the Lord leading me to put all that He had revealed to me in one place as a source of hope and encouragement for those of you who are about to enter a significant period of waiting, for those of you who are in the middle of one now, and for those of you who are loving someone else through a period of waiting.

Dawson Trotman said, "Thoughts disentangle themselves when they pass through our fingertips."[1] So, I hope, in this case, that the many thoughts that have been sprinting through my head over the last few years do become disentangled as they pass through my fingertips onto the words of these pages. It is my sincere prayer that at least one of those thoughts that found its way into this book will be helpful to you.

I have traveled down this road you are walking, and I know how excruciatingly difficult it is. I know that many people don't understand what you are going through, but I do. My heart breaks for the struggle and the frustration that each day can represent for you. Yet, my heart soars for all I know that God will teach you during this time and how He will love you in ways that you have never been loved before.

We are on this journey together, and I promise that is not a dead end! Eventually, our waiting will come to an end, we will see God's purpose in the process, and we will find that the blessings of obediently waiting for God will leave us simply breathless.

By God's Grace,

Rachel

Chapter 1

Waiting

We All Have Periods of Waiting

We all will have periods of waiting in our lives. That is a given! But before we dive into this perplexing topic, let's agree to define waiting as the action of staying where we are or delaying our action for a particular time.[2]

Even in this age of modern technology and conveniences, waiting is still a big part of every one of our lives. You may start your day off by waiting for your coffee to brew. If you live in an area of high congestion like I do, you typically start off your trek into work by waiting in traffic. You may get to work only to continue to wait on your boss's decision about a project you are working on. You will probably wait at a restaurant for lunch. You might have to wait in line to pick up your kids from school. You will probably wait on a service repairman to repair your broken washing machine or other major appliance, especially if they give you the lovely "window" of four or five hours for their arrival. And it would be a small miracle if you did not have to wait in line at the grocery store. Of course, you will absolutely have to wait in an airport terminal for your flight to board. The bottom line is you will wait in this life.

I would label these moments as our momentary, fleeting, or short-lived waiting events. Although they can be somewhat trying, we know approximately when our waiting will end. And their ending usually comes within a few minutes or a few hours, within the day, or within the week in which they occur. With these waiting events, we see the light at the end of the tunnel (and it doesn't appear to be an oncoming train).

On the opposite side of the spectrum, we have our continuing, long-lasting, or enduring waiting events. These events carry with them a far heavier emotional burden, and in some cases, a burden so heavy it is difficult to make it through the day. These events are not kind enough to be short-lived but rather last for days, weeks, months, and yes, even years.

You may find yourself in a job situation that's beyond difficult to endure, and you do not know how much longer you can survive waiting for the conditions or the management to change. You may be out of a job and currently waiting on responses from the fifty resumes and applications you sent out. Perhaps you are having health issues and waiting for the pain to finally subside. It could be that you are single and waiting for Mr. or Ms. Right to finally come into your life. Or perhaps, you are waiting to finally become a parent, whether that occurs through your own pregnancy or through adoption.

I don't know what your situation is, but I do know how heavy the burden is. And I do know how hard waiting is. I know that because I have personally been there, and I understand the spiritual battle that can ensue. Unfortunately, we are a part of fallen humanity, and our natural tendency is to take matters into our own hands, to fix what is broken, and to follow our own paths. So, our natural tendency is not to "wait on the Lord," resulting in an internal war of sorts when He asks us to wait on Him. At best, it's uncomfortable, and at worst, it's excruciatingly painful, as what we are collides with what God wants us to be.

What Does It Mean to Wait on the Lord

So, what does it mean to wait on the Lord? To wait on the Lord is to look to Him in expectation and to eagerly anticipate what He is about to do. It sounds so easy, right? I can look to the Lord in expectation of bringing my waiting to closure, and yes, I am eagerly anticipating what He is about to do and when He is about to do it. And yet, when that waiting lasts day after day, week after week, month after month, year after year, it is one of the hardest things the Lord will ever ask us to do.

It's not just about the waiting either. It's often about *what* we are waiting for, as we wait for different things at different times in our lives. Sometimes we are waiting for direction from God. Sometimes we are waiting for doors to be opened that only He has the power to open. Sometimes we are waiting for extremely murky and confusing situations to come clear. And sometimes we are waiting for the deepest needs and longings of our hearts to finally be fulfilled by God.

The one constant in all our waiting on the Lord is the passage of time. In Psalm 130:5-6, the psalmist writes, "I wait for the LORD, my whole being waits, and in His word I put my hope. I wait for the Lord more than watchmen wait for the morning, more than watchmen wait for the morning."[3]

The psalmist is comparing his own waiting to that of the night watchmen who eagerly anticipated the coming dawn of morning as that would signify their release from duty. The watchmen knew that the dawn would surely come, but it would only come with the passing of time. It is in the same way that we eagerly await the passing of time to bring our release from our waiting period.

During this time of waiting, we often have the *opportunity* (said with a very large smile on my face) to surrender our timing to God's timing. We have the most wonderful ideas about when something in our lives should occur—down to the date and the time. I know I have been even so bold, and yes, naïve, to share those wonderful ideas with the Lord. In fact, at this point in my life, I firmly believed and shared with the Lord that I would have a loving husband who I had been married to at least ten years, two well-behaved kids—a boy and a girl, an awesome dog, and a great home. Well...I have the great dog and home, but apparently, my timing on the other desires of my heart was *way* off.

More often than not, however, our ideas on timing are light years apart from God's plans. So, we must surrender to His timing, and when we do, He can do amazing things in us and for us. The hard part is reminding ourselves that God acts on behalf of those who wait for Him. In fact, the Bible tells us, "Since ancient times no one has heard, no ear has perceived, no eye has seen any God besides you, who acts on behalf of those who wait for Him."[4]

Although the waiting is excruciatingly difficult and seems pointless, our waiting is never useless. Let me repeat that point because I think it is just that important! Although the waiting is excruciatingly difficult and seems pointless, our waiting is never useless! God is working behind the scenes, and things are happening that we cannot even begin to fathom.

It's as if our lives are the threads making up a beautiful tapestry. We often can only see the underside of the tapestry, which is messy, with threads connected here and there in seemingly no rhyme or reason. Some threads even seem to disappear into a dead end. But God has the design of the tapestry of our lives ever at the forefront of His mind. Each and every thread has a perfect place and has a purpose within the tapestry. When the tapestry is finally turned over and God reveals His work, we will finally understand how every single thread of our lives came together to present the most breathtaking picture.

But far too often, we want to help the Lord with the weaving of tapestry because we are impatient. We don't want to wait for Him to finish the last few threads on the tapestry or to tie the last few knots, so we grab it off the loom before it is completed. We don't want to wait for Him to ripen the fruit, and so we pick it while it is still green. We don't want to wait for the answers to our prayers, so we move ahead in the way we think is right. Our impatience and restlessness only result in one thing: more trouble in our lives. Our human interference will result in one outcome; it will make things messier than they already are, and it will exhaust us in the process.

Although our natural tendencies cry out for movement, we must will ourselves to wait. (And you have no idea how hard this is for me to say as a self-professed "get-to-it" kind of girl.) You and I must listen ever so closely to that still quiet voice (that I often wish was a still medium or still loud voice) of the Holy Spirit, guiding us in the way that we should go. We need to accept what the Lord is doing in our lives and trust Him to fulfill His perfect will for our lives. We need to wait with purposeful anticipation of God accomplishing all that He has promised.

> When I cannot understand my Father's leading,
> And it seems to be but hard and cruel fate,
> Still I hear that gentle whisper ever pleading,
> God is working, God is faithful,
> Only wait.[5]

Waiting for the Desires of Our Hearts

God-Given Desires

One of the hardest things to do is to wait for the deepest desires and longings of our hearts to be fulfilled. We know that God is the Giver of Dreams and the One who has placed desires deep inside each one of our hearts. He has given us gifts, skills, and talents that we dream about using in different ways. He even gives us dreams about our future in terms of relationships and family.

I am convinced that God allows desires to rise up at different times in different seasons of our lives. When we think about it, God perfectly times those desires in our lives. As an example, when we were in high school, many of us had a desire to have fun, get good grades, and participate in different school activities. We weren't focused on landing the right job, finding our mate, buying a house, or starting a family. Those types of desires would come, but they would come at the right time and in the right season.

Sometimes the season is quickly upon us, and our desires hit with such urgency it is hard to fathom. It is almost as if the Lord literally allows them to be awakened out of a deep sleep. And we cry out to the Lord to have those desires met.

I believe there is a process that we often go through that I will label the Cycle of Desires (Figure 1) that begins with those God-given desires.

Figure 1: Cycle of Desires

God's Promises

Our God-given desires are bolstered by God's promises. Psalm 37:4 says, "Take delight in the Lord, and He will give you the desires of your heart."[6] This is God's precious promise to us: when we delight ourselves in Him, He will give us the very desires of our heart.

Psalm 145:19 reiterates that promise by telling us that "He fulfills the desires of those who fear Him."[7] I have always been encouraged by the fact that both verses use the word "desires" and not the word "desire." I would hate to have to narrow my desire list down to one or two favorites!

But I am even more encouraged by the fact that no desire is ever placed in us by the Holy Spirit unless He intends to fulfill it. He isn't putting desires in our hearts just so He can squash our hopes and dreams like little bugs. No! He breathes heavenly life into our hearts, so we continue to look forward with hope to the fulfillment of those things we long for the most.

We have a perfect example of God delivering on His Promises with Abraham. God promised Abraham in Genesis 12:1-2 that he would be the father of a "great nation," and yet months turned into years with no sign of fatherhood on the horizon.[8] Eventually, Abraham bore a son with Hagar, but God again told him in Genesis 15:4, "This man will not be your heir, but a son who is your own flesh and blood will be your heir."[9] Again, more years passed by with no son. At this point, the Lord called out to Abraham and said, "Look up at the sky and count the stars—if indeed you can count them...[s]o shall your offspring be."[10]

The years continue to drag on, and at this point, Abraham is hundred years old and Sarai, his wife, is ninety years old. Now granted, people lived very long lives back in this era. Even with that in mind, the ninety-to-one-hundred age range would not classify a ninety-year-old as a "spring chicken." In fact, at this point in her life, Sarai was medically unable to bear a child.

But God, perhaps knowing how human doubt can creep in, again returned to Abraham and said, "As for Sarai your wife, you are no longer to call her Sarai; her name will be Sarah. I will bless her and will surely give you a son by her. I will bless her so that she will be the mother of nations; kings of peoples will come from her."[11]

Not only was God specific about the bloodline that would come from Sarah's womb, but He was also specific about the *who* and the *when*. In terms of the *who*, God had specific instructions for Abraham regarding the boy's name, saying, "your wife Sarah will bear you a son, and you will call him Isaac."[12] In terms of the *when*, God was even specific in the timing, saying, "I will surely return to you at the appointed time next year and Sarah will have a son."[13]

In all, God came to Abraham four different times to reinforce His Promise for Abraham's future. And those promises all came true...down to the very last detail. Even when everything looked bleak and the sun had set on what was medically possible, God's promise was a guarantee.

Waiting

God's Promises are a signed, sealed guarantee, but often so is the waiting that accompanies them. Like we see with Abraham, sometimes God gives us promises far in advance of their fulfillment to give us hope for our future and stability during our present pain. But He still makes us wait and wait and wait for them—to the point we honestly believe our hearts will explode with anxiety or pain. See, it's in our hearts where our deepest desires reside, and therefore it is the most vulnerable of places for us.

But because those desires are in the most vulnerable places and are often the most important to us, they are also of utmost importance to God. And He is never inactive in our waiting time, even when He calls us to be still. In fact, He absolutely loves to work for those who will wait for Him.

Although He may not explain all His purposes to us as He has us in this season of waiting, there is always a reason. I am sure that Abraham would have gladly relived every day of waiting, knowing the joy that his son Isaac brought him for the rest of his days. Even though the waiting felt like an eternity, Isaac was worth waiting for.

God has something worth us waiting for too. I was driving to a function the other day and praying while I drove. Much of the time spent driving involves me praying that I don't get a ticket (I tend to think of speed limits as guidelines), but on this particular trip, I was bearing my soul to the Lord in terms of my desires and longing for a family. And that's when the Lord laid it on my heart, "I am making you wait because there is something worth waiting for." There is something worth waiting for. It's kind of hard to argue with that, and so I have no choice but to wait.

There are days I feel much like I am sure Sarai felt: a bit past my prime in terms of the timeline of my hopes and dreams, a bit on the wrong side of where I would like to be. But that's when God does something to remind me of the promises He has given me. That's when He reminds me that my waiting will produce a joy that I will carry with me for the rest of my life.

Surrender

No matter how much we convince ourselves it will all be worth the wait, we often get to the point where the pain of waiting for our desires to come to fruition literally brings us to our knees. We get to the point we just want to give up. It is here in the Cycle of Desires, we can become bitter and angry, or we can surrender our desires and future dreams to the Lord who already knows what will be best for us. Although it appears to be a simple and logical choice, surrendering can be something we battle daily.

Surrendering our desires and dreams to the Lord is really the second act of this drama. The first key act involves us surrendering our very lives to the Lord. The bottom line is God loves each one of us and has a plan for our lives. In fact, He loved us so much that as John 3:16 tells us, "God so loved the world that He gave His one and only Son, that whoever believes in Him shall not perish, but have eternal life."[14]

Unfortunately, we are sinners, and our sin separates us from God. Romans 3:23 tells us, "All have sinned and fall short of the glory of God."[15] Romans 6:23 goes on to tell us the consequences of our sin:

"For the wages of sin is death, but the gift of God is eternal life in Christ Jesus our Lord."[16]

God's gift was in the form of Jesus Christ, the only provision for our sins. Jesus Christ died on the cross for our sins so that the gulf between God and us could be bridged. Through Him and Him alone can we know and experience God's love for us and ultimate plan for our lives. Romans 5:8 tells us, "But God demonstrates His own love for us in this: While we were still sinners, Christ died for us."[17] Not only did Christ die for us, but He literally defeated death by dying on the cross, being buried, and being raised from the dead on the third day.

To fully experienced God's loved and plan for our lives, we must individually receive Jesus Christ as our Lord and Savior. In Revelation 3:20, Jesus says, "Behold, I stand at the door and knock. If anyone hears My voice and opens the door, I will come in to him."[18] All we have to do is open the door of our hearts, knowing in faith that this is a gift we have done nothing to earn. "For by grace you have been saved through faith, and that not of yourselves; it is the gift of God; not of works, lest anyone should boast."[19]

Opening the door to your heart is as simple as praying a prayer such as this:

"Lord Jesus, I need you. I know I am a sinner. Thank You for dying on the cross for my sins so that I may spend eternity with You. Today, I open the door of my heart and ask You to be my Lord and Savior. Thank You for forgiving me and loving me. Take my life and use it in whatever manner will bring glory and honor to You."

It is truly that simple and truly that life-changing. My prayer is that if you have not made that commitment to Christ or prayed a similar prayer to this one, that today you will. Make today the day you change your life forever. Surrender your heart to the Lord and watch with amazement at the things He will do in your life.

God's Blessings

As we turn back again to the Cycle of Desires, where we are at the point of "Giving Up" and "Surrendering," God seems to open up His storehouse of blessings and rains them down in a way that literally blows our minds. He wants to bless us abundantly. In fact, John 10:10 says, "I have come that they might have life, and that they may have it more abundantly."[20]

Full Cycle of Desires

What a cycle to take us through! I don't understand why we have to go through it, but from my perspective, there appear to be two key points: 1. God wants to bring us to the point where we know we need Him more than anything else in this life; and 2. God wants to bring us to the point of brokenness and submission where we are willing to do and be anything He wants us to do and be!

The beauty in the Cycle of Desires is that, thankfully, dreams don't come with expiration dates. Dreams don't spoil just because they are a year or two old. And just because we may take what we think of as a detour to get to our final destination, these alternative routes come as no surprise to God. Instead, you may very well find that the detour is the very method God is using to move you toward a dream perfected for you. The experiences and the wisdom you gain along the longer road may make your dream that much sweeter, and in fact, that may prove to be the purpose of the delay all along. Just keep patiently waiting. God is far from finished with your dreams.

And remember, nothing is too hard for the Lord. As He did with Abraham and Sarah, He loves to pull off the impossible. No matter how long you have waited or how impossible your situation looks, stay faithful. Your time is coming. God has put these dreams in your heart, and He has given you these promises. He has every intention of bringing it to pass. So, take heart and know what a sense of joy He must get as He orchestrates miracles in the lives of those who love Him.

Waiting is a Choice

The reality in all of this is that waiting is a choice. Now mind you, it isn't an easy choice, but it is our choice to make. What I have found during my own period of waiting was that it wasn't a choice I made once, but rather a choice that I had to make over and over and over again, minute by minute, hour by hour.

When I say that it's a choice, I mean that when we know God is calling us to wait for something, someone, or some situation to change, we can either: Ignore Him, Disobey Him, or Obey Him. In Ignoring Him, we can literally choose to simply disregard what He is telling us to do. We can just stop listening to Him, or when we start to hear Him directing us, we can quickly tune Him out. I see this regularly happen with my dog, Kallie, when I ask her to do something she is simply not interested in doing. Now, I will put a disclaimer out there that she truly is an angel, but she too has her moments. When she is having one of those moments, she simply turns her head away from me like she never heard me. And we often do the same with God. If I haven't heard Him, then I don't have to do what He is telling me to do.

We can also Disobey God. We can know exactly what He wants us to do—wait, for example, for that new job—but we willfully choose to reject His direction and take a job we believe is a "good fit." This attitude is full of arrogance and pride and essentially is saying to God, "I know far more than You do about what is best for me and my life."

Or, we can Obey Him. God has a specific plan for each one of our lives that is tailor-made for just us. No two lives are designed according to the same pattern. And here, I want to specifically call out the fact that no one else can know what God is calling you to do. When God asked Noah to build an ark, He didn't have a conference call with the rest of Noah's friends and family to fill them in on the "Big Vision Ark plan." No, He told Noah and Noah alone. So those around you may not, and probably will not, understand or comprehend what God is calling you to do. In fact, they may downright disagree, but we are not accountable to them in the end. We are accountable to our Heavenly Father.

When we step out in obedience and make that choice to obey God and to wait, then God reveals the next step and the next and the next. Here, again, this is not easy! In fact, learning to wait on God and His perfect timing can be one of the most frustrating things we ever encounter in our walk with Him. (Especially for those who are planners and like to know what is coming a bit in advance!) But we must trust and know that God not only knows best about the what He is going to bring into our lives, but He also knows the best *when*.

We have all heard that timing is everything. But when it comes to our lives, timing really is everything. I absolutely love to bake cookies and use my Granny Sue Sue's chocolate chip cookie recipe that I know by heart. When I was first learning to make the recipe, there were times I left the cookies in for too long and they burned. Other times I pulled them out just a bit too early and they were too gooey. After years of making the cookies, I know the exact amount of time to make the cookies moist and soft on the inside and just a bit firmer on the outside. Timing is everything.

God knows the exact timing of the "cookies" He wants to give us. He has so many "cookies" in store for us it will take a lifetime for us to eat them all. But we must wait on His timing for each one because if we don't, we may just end up with a gooey pile of mush.

We are in good company, though, as we look at major figures in the Bible who were forced to wait long periods of time before God brought them to a place of success. Abraham waited twenty-five years from the time God promised him a son to the time Sarah gave birth to Isaac. Joseph endured thirteen years of betrayal by his family, false accusations, and false imprisonment before becoming the second in command in Egypt. Moses suffered through forty years of tending sheep before God called him to serve as the very deliverer of His people. Finally, David battled through fourteen years from the time he was anointed as the future King of Israel until the time he assumed the throne of Israel.

The experience of these individuals reminds us all that waiting is not incidental to faith but is rather the very DNA of faith. Times of waiting can be the most grueling of life's seasons, but they can also be the times we can refine our skills for what He has next. So, let's make the choice to wait no matter how difficult our season of waiting becomes.

Chapter 2

The Difficulty of Waiting

I wish I could tell you that waiting is easy. But it's not. There are moments of darkness and despair that are all-encompassing. But the light will shine through again. There are moments of pain and suffering that seem unbearable. But you can make it. There are times when it appears that the trial of your waiting will continue forever. But it won't. I promise.

In the meantime, my purpose in writing this chapter was to provide you with hope and insight as you enter those times of darkness, despair, pain, suffering, and facing what feels like a never-ending trial. During my own waiting periods, there were days that I didn't think I could take one more step, and then God would provide some amazing encouragement on the Internet, through a song on the way to work, in a devotional that just captured exactly what I was feeling, or through a family member or friend's words of encouragement. Those moments of light gave me that little bit of hope I needed to keep pressing on. My prayer is that this chapter does the same for you.

The Darkness of Waiting

I had no idea, no idea whatsoever just how dark the waiting period could be or would be. During my most difficult periods of waiting, it seemed that a cloud would literally descend on my heart out of nowhere, and everything would suddenly look bleak and dark.

During these times, I realized I was struggling to hold on to what little hope I had left. In some cases, I am sorry to say, I did lose all hope that what I was waiting for would ever occur. It was so dark that I felt like I was literally waiting for hope. There were times I saw no hint of success, but I refused to let the despair overtake me. Like a kickboxer, I often felt like I was in the ring with despair. I won some rounds, and despair won a few rounds as well. The key was, though, that every time I got knocked down, I kept getting back up. Despair was not going to win, and I was not going to let the empty place in my heart be filled with anything but God's best. Period. No settling.

But there were times it was so dark that I found myself struggling to believe in God's goodness. In my head, I logically knew that God is good, and I had all the Bible story knowledge to prove it. But to go from head to heart when your heart is shattering into a million pieces is a different story altogether. I mean, did He really see the darkness that engulfed me? Did He care that the darkness was choking out the last little bit of hope I had? Could He see that I was having difficulty picking myself up off the mat for the fiftieth time?

The hardest part of the darkness was feeling like it would never end. I found that when I was in that dark time, I started to project it into the future. The longer I persevered through difficult circumstances, the darker the path ahead seemed to become and the harder it was to see even a flicker of light ever shining on that path again.

Satan loves to get us to this point. He wants more than anything for us to just give up and let misery and darkness become our constant companions. However, I have found that darkness and misery are not the best road trip companions and that if I have to be trucking down waiting road, I would far rather be trucking down that road with the God of the Universe as my companion. He is the One who knows my every need and who loves me unconditionally. I place my trust in Him.

> Who among you fears the LORD
> and obeys the word of his servant?
> Let the one who walks in the dark,

who has no light,
trust in the name of the LORD
and rely on their God.[21]

Staying in the Darkness until It Ends

Although ever so tempting—especially when we can *do* something to get out of the dark place—we need to stay there until God brings it to an end in His time and in His way. He knows exactly what we are going through, and He is teaching us lessons that we desperately need to know. Our interference will only circumvent the much-needed work in our lives that this time of darkness is facilitating.

The emperor moth provides us a great example of how the struggles we endure in the darkness are so necessary. The emperor moth is one of the most majestic species among all the moths. It has wide wings that span out gloriously when it flies.

Before the emperor moth can achieve this grandiosity, it must begin its life as a pupa in a cocoon. The neck of that cocoon is extremely narrow, and it is narrow for a purpose. In order for it to become a moth with this beautiful wingspan, the pupa must first squeeze its way out of the narrow neck. This process allows for the blood in the body of the pupa to be pushed into the wings, thus completing their transformation.

One day a man found a cocoon of an emperor moth. He took it home so that he could watch the moth come out of the cocoon. He sat and watched the moth struggling to force the body through that little hole. Then it seemed to stop making any progress. It appeared as if it had gotten as far as it could, and it could go no farther. It just seemed to be stuck.

Then the man being kind decided to help the moth. So, he took a pair of scissors and snipped off the remaining bit of the cocoon. The moth then emerged easily. But it had a swollen body and small, shriveled wings. He expected that the wings would enlarge and expand to be able to support the body, which would contract in time. Neither happened! In fact, the little moth spent the rest of its life crawling around with a swollen body and shriveled wings. It never was able to fly. A few days later, it died.

What the man in his kindness and haste did not understand was that the restricting cocoon and the struggle required for the moth to get through the tiny opening was the way of forcing fluid from the body of the moth into its wings so that it would be ready for flight once it achieved its freedom from the cocoon. Freedom and flight would only come after the struggle. By depriving the moth of a struggle, he deprived the emperor moth of health.[22]

You see, sometimes the struggles we face in the darkest of days are necessary to squeeze the kind of character into us that we need to spread our "majestic wings" and bring glory to God. But we have to stop interfering with God's plan, stop trying to pull out the scissors to snip the cocoon, and stop trying to move the hands of time to better suit our preferences. The bottom line is that we may be able to move the hands of the clock, but that doesn't mean we have actually changed the time.

And beyond the lessons that God wants to teach us and the character that He wants to build in us, He also takes us into the darkness to give us the treasure of knowledge of Himself. God says to us, "I will give you the treasures of darkness and hidden wealth of secret places, So that you may know that it is I, The Lord, The God of Israel, who calls you by your name."[23]

Sometimes the experience and discipline of darkness is the only place where He can teach us to listen and hear Him. It is in the darkness that He tells us secrets. Secrets that were only meant to be known between the two of us. Secrets that we are blinded to in the glare of daylight.

What we realize as He whispers His Secrets to us is that He is right there in the darkness with us. He is right there in the midst of our darkest place. When we feel the most lonely and forsaken, He is near.

The storms of sorrow felt in the darkness are intense, but they are one of God's ways of driving us back to Him. And when we wrap our arms around Him as we tremble with fear of what is around us and what is to come, He speaks softly and tenderly to our hearts. We will feel His love during the storm because we know, "Jesus Christ is not my security against the storms of life, but He is my perfect security in the storms."[24]

So, when the storms close in on us and the darkness surrounds us, we must bind ourselves to Him. Our own reasoning will fail us. Our past experiences may shed little light on our current predicament. And sometimes, even prayer brings us no consolation. We must anchor ourselves "steadfastly upon the Lord. And then, come what may— whether wind, waves, rough seas, thunder, lightning, jagged rocks, or roaring breaker" we must lash ourselves to the "helm, firmly holding your confidence in God's faithfulness, His covenant promises."[25]

God Works in the Darkness

The hardest part about the darkness in waiting is that nothing seems to be happening. We seem to be suspended in time, feeling like life is moving all around us, but we are standing still in quicksand. We don't understand what's going on or why we must wait for so long. Often, we are unable to see any possible good arising from our waiting experience.

But God is at work in the darkness. We may see absolutely no evidence yet, but God is at work. He is at work just like He was for the Israelites as we see in Exodus 14:21, "...and all that night the Lord drove the sea back..."[26] God works through the night until the morning light when dawn breaks, and our waiting comes to an end.

In the darkness, He is drawing us closer to Him, weaving the crazy strands of our lives together into His purposes.

If He has given you a vision or promise of what is to come, wait, and He will bring that vision to fulfillment in His perfect timing. He may keep you waiting in the darkness, but He always remembers His promises, and His word will never be broken. He has the resources and the resourcefulness to bring His promises to fruition in the most miraculous of ways, even in the most difficult of situations. "Difficulty is actually the atmosphere surrounding a miracle or a miracle in its initial stage. Yet if it is to be a great miracle, the surrounding condition will be not simply a difficulty but an utter impossibility."[27]

So, when the darkness closes in and the situation looks utterly impossible, know God is at work. "Sit quietly. Breathe deeply. Hope steadily. God is working on your behalf this very moment."[28]

Our Darkness Will Come to an End

Our darkness will come to an end. Let me say that again. Our darkness will come to an end. We will not stay in this period of darkness forever, although it undoubtedly feels like it. Every night is followed by dawn, and our dark waiting period will be followed by its own dawn of blessings. When we are "faithful to forge ahead and 'if we do not give up,'[29] someday we will know that the most exquisite work of our lives was done during those days when it was the darkest."[30]

Thankfully, God in His great compassion often blesses us with streaks of light that break through the darkness—providing hope and comfort. Those streaks of light seem like they were beamed directly down from heaven in the form of an encouraging word from a friend, the sermon of a pastor, or even things that God puts directly in your path that you simply cannot miss that confirm His will for your life.

So often for me, those streaks of light have come in the way of my devotionals. I will cry out to the Lord at night, just emptying my heart of its hurt, only to find that my devotional the next morning is speaking directly to what I vented. Coincidence? Hardly! Those streaks of light have also come in the form of Christian songs as I am driving to and from work. It just seems that God allows the perfect song with the perfect words to speak to my hurting heart at just the right time. Again coincidence? Not a chance!

The streaks of light are there to remind us that even when the darkness hides the sun, it doesn't extinguish it. Although the darkness may hide the stars, the stars still shine brilliantly once again. We simply must wait for the darkness to fall away and for the light of the sun and the brilliance of the stars to shine once more on our upturned faces.

So, don't give up right before the darkness falls away. As Charles Spurgeon once said, "The wilderness is the way to Canaan. Defeat prepares us for victory. The darkest hour of the night precedes the dawn." Remember that in your darkest hour, dawn is coming, and there will be light. And the harder the darkness is to bear, the more likely it will bring blessings from God that we cannot even begin to imagine.

Let God's mercy hold you in the darkness. Know that the darkness is simply holding back a brilliant sunrise. And let God light each step of your way, even when you can't see the next step ahead, to the breaking of the dawn and the beautiful promises He has in store just for you.

The Despair in Waiting

The despair in waiting can be crippling. I know firsthand. I am a passionate person but tend not to be what I would call a "crier." However, during my time of waiting, I cried—when I say cried, I should say wept, sobbed, melted—more days than I did not. There were literally days that something would hit me, and I would sink to the floor of my bedroom in a heap of tears with the weight of despair holding me down for what seemed like an eternity.

In moments of clarity, I am surprised that I have made it this far. In all honesty, when the despair would hit me like a Mack truck, there were days that, like Job, I begged for the Lord to either end my misery or to just take me home to be with Him. Perhaps you, too, have had these moments when you have called out to God in anguish, begging for mercy from your misery, and He just doesn't seem to be answering. Despair drains the last ounce of hope out of you, and you are simply too exhausted to "fight the good fight" one more day.

David felt that way too, and the Psalms drip with his tears of anguish as he cries out to the Lord in his own despair.

> Save me, O God,
> for the waters have come up to my neck,
> I sink in the miry depths,
> Where there is no foothold.
> I have come into the deep waters;
> The floods engulf me.
> I am worn out calling for help;
> My throat is parched.
> My eyes fail,
> Looking for my God.[31]

> Lord, you are the God who saves me;
> Day and night I cry out to you.
> May my prayer come before you;
> Turn your ear to my cry.
> I am overwhelmed with troubles
> And my life draws near to death.[32]

While we wait on God, our hearts often ask, "Why? Why is all this necessary? Why must I hurt to the core of who I am?" Our spirits are consumed with hopelessness, and we start to wonder if God is truly trustworthy in fulfilling His promises. Doubt presses in from every angle, wreaking havoc on our hearts and minds.

But we cannot give in to despair because once it has taken us under, fighting our way back to the surface will be beyond challenging. It's like riding the waves at the beach, and suddenly, a big wave suddenly takes you under. The water just seems to churn you back under over and over again, and you can't seem to break loose to find your way back up for air. It's like you are caught in a never-ending cycle. Despair, if we give in to it, will put us in the same churn cycle that will be even more difficult to escape.

Job even mentions this "churn" in his own heart when he says in Job 30:26-27:

> Yet when I hoped for good, evil came;
> when I looked for light, then came darkness.
> The churning inside me never stops;
> days of suffering confront me.[33]

Falling into this churn of despair is a dangerous cycle. Satan has made it so subtle that at times we start slipping into despair without even realizing it. Hope is ever so slowly replaced by hopelessness as we take our eyes off God's blessings in our everyday lives. As hope withers away, it leaves ground for despair to begin to take root. When despair takes root, the normal adversities we face in life become exaggerated, and our burden becomes seemingly too heavy for us to bear.

Why would Satan use this tactic? Satan uses the despair tactic because it is difficult for the Lord to work with a crushed soul. Our eyes become so focused on our own dire circumstances that we find it impossible to pick them up and gaze upon the One who can save us.

When we lose hope, we forget that God Himself is guiding our steps even through our most difficult times. Now, if we believe that He is directing every step of our lives, then it follows that He has allowed us to come into this very place from which we cry out for mercy. He has permitted the circumstances that brought us to our knees. We don't know the plan or purpose of it all, but He does.

David was very aware of this as he wrote in Psalm 71:20,

> Though you have made me see troubles,
> Many and bitter,
> You will restore my life again;
> From the depths of the earth
> You will again bring me up.[34]

Part of our despair, at least I know for myself, is that I find the waiting time to be such a useless place. I am a "to-do" list kind of girl, and so being in a place of waiting—especially for long periods of time—makes me feel useless and as if every second waiting is a second wasted. But again, God uses these waiting times in our lives for specific purposes. We can trust that He will not allow us to remain in this waiting period one second longer than it takes to accomplish those specific purposes.

What makes it all so hard is that sometimes even those seconds feel like an eternity. So, what do we do to keep ourselves from falling headlong into the pit of despair? At risk of sounding too simplistic, we need to do three things. First, we need to look for the silver lining in the current clouds above us. Secondly, we need to look ahead to brighter times in the future. And third, we need to remind ourselves that God's timing is perfect and wait patiently on the Lord. Let's dive into these in a little more detail.

The first thing we need to do is to look for the silver lining in the current clouds around us. They may be the most minimal things in the world, but we have to start somewhere. For instance, during my time of waiting, I realized that I had far more time to read. And boy, did I read! In fact, when I look back at that particular period of time, I realized I was reading four to five books a month. I was reading all different types of books, and I loved it. I recognize now that I may never have another period like that in my life.

Once we find those silver linings, we need to find ways to remind ourselves what they are...which in our despair can become a very difficult task. In my times of despair, I have also found the silver linings to be specific promises and verses from God. When I ran across them in my devotional time or in my Bible study or even in my pastor's sermons, I wrote each one in a small spiral notebook that I took everywhere. My goal was to memorize each one of them. That way, when Satan began his subtle despair attacks, I recited those verses either out loud or in my head depending on where I was and rebuked those attacks.

Secondly, with eyes of faith, we need to look ahead through the darkness to brighter times in the future. As we already discussed, our time of darkness *will* end—we just don't know *when*. So, we need to praise God for those brighter times that are coming and continue to persevere until the light that streaks through every now and then becomes a brilliant stream of light.

As David wrote, "I would have despaired unless I had believed that I would see the goodness of the Lord in the land of the living."[35] David focused on seeing the brighter times "in the land of the living." Let's be clear here. David was beating his despair by recognizing that he would see God's goodness while he was still alive. His focus was on seeing God's blessings in his life on earth and not just the goodness of the Lord in heaven.

Thirdly, we need to remind ourselves that God's timing is perfect and wait patiently for the Lord. When Habakkuk was falling into despair because he didn't think God was acting quickly enough, God had this to say to him, "For the revelation awaits an appointed time...though it linger, wait for it; it will certainly come and will not delay."[36] God pointed out that everything has an appointed time, and although Habakkuk may have thought the time was lingering, lagging, or at times even moving backwards (*Amen!*), God assured him the revelation would come with no delay in God's timeline.

Unfortunately, though, when we are in the throes of despair, there is a weariness that sets in. There were times during my own waiting period when I found myself feeling physically weak. During those times, I wanted to curl up under my covers in my bed and sleep through an entire week, just hoping that the next week would bring an end to the waiting. As a teenager, my parents would sometimes joke that they were going to "knock us into next week." During my time of waiting, I can assure you that there were times I would gladly have taken them up on that offer!

God knows and understands how despair can bring bone weariness because He knows us. So, He doesn't ask us to "[b]e strong and courageous" during times like this.[37] Instead, He says gently, "Be still, and know that I am God."[38] Rather than trying to be strong during this time, we can simply lean on the shoulder of the One who loves us more than we know. We can become still and trust in His strength when we have none. We can let God pull us into His arms and love us back onto to our feet and out from under those covers.

Take heart, and God will lovingly come to us in our heaps of despair. We live in a world full of storms—both figuratively and literally. And the hurt and pain can drive us into hopelessness. When we are stumbling headlong into pits of despair, it's hard to see, feel, or believe in hope.

But God sent His Son, Jesus, as our very hope and salvation. Jesus gently and carefully helps us out of the pit. And in His love, our hope is renewed. Because let's be honest, God does His best work when the situations are hopeless, when we are faced with the impossible, and when we have nowhere else to turn but Him.

The Pain of Waiting

A friend of mine recently reminded me of the well-known quote by Daniel J. Evans, "Pain is a sign of weakness leaving the body." He then said, "The funny thing about that quote is, I've never seemed to run out of weakness." That makes two of us! And I would say that is rather a perfect way to describe the pain of waiting...you just never seem to run out of pain.

I am not sure I can adequately put the pain of waiting into words. But during my hardest time of waiting, I wrote this in one of my journals:

"Yesterday was one of the roughest days I have had in a long time. It felt like everything was crashing in. The depth of the pain in my heart is just indescribable—it's always there—no matter what I do, it just doesn't go away. No amount of prayer or verse memory or anything helps. It's just a constant pain.

"But last night, the pain welled up inside and just about drowned me. I was having book club at my house, and I felt it creeping up on me—and then I was just counting the seconds before the ladies would leave because I knew that the minute they did, I would be balling.

"They barely made it out of my front door before the tears were just streaming down my face. And the tears didn't stop for about an hour. I couldn't make them stop.

"Now, I have finally figured out that the shower is a great place to cry. I don't understand the science behind it, but I know that when I cry in the shower, my eyes are far less puffy and red than they are when I cry someplace else. So, into the shower I ran. And the tears ran down my face until there were so many tears that I no longer needed the water from the shower to wash away my hurt."

Now the pain of my water bill increasing after coming across the magic of the shower on erasing puffy eyes was palatable, but the pain found in the hearts of those of us who are in a period of waiting is far worse. Why is it so painful? It is gut-wrenchingly painful because our hope is being deferred. The very desires of our heart that we daily hope and pray for are still unrealized. And I truly believe that the deeper the desire is lodged into our hearts, the deeper the pain will be until that desire is realized.

When the pain hits us the hardest, we are even tempted to doubt that God really knows what He is doing or if perhaps He's simply causing us to endure unnecessary pain. There is a lovely saying that goes something along the lines of "God never gives us more than we can handle." Well, in my times of deepest pain, I have often thought that God simply mixed me up with someone else. He was thinking of a far stronger person, and unfortunately, I got zapped with their share of pain. I would readily return it to God, or to the super person, for what I know was my far more manageable share of pain, but I quickly found out that God doesn't have a return or exchange policy.

God didn't have me mixed up with anyone else, and He doesn't have a mix-up going on in your life. He knows exactly what we are going through, and He knows exactly what He is doing. He knows it because He is right there in the middle of the pain with us. Psalm 34:18 tells us, "The Lord is close to the brokenhearted and saves those who are crushed in spirit."[39] Brokenhearted—check. Crushed in spirit—check, check. Are you there too? Then the Lord is close, and He is there to save us!

Psalm 147:3 speaks again of the brokenhearted and says, "He heals the brokenhearted and binds up their wounds."[40] God knows that our deepest pain in life will come from our hearts being broken through disappointment and waiting with hope for something that seems to be so far away. He gets it, and He is right there, not just to glue the pieces back together but to make a brand new, transformed heart out of the wreckage of our pain.

See, pain can bring forth life and joy. In fact, sometimes joy needs pain to give birth. John 16:20-23 says, "Very truly I tell you, you will weep and mourn while the world rejoices. You will grieve, but your grief will turn to joy. A woman giving birth to a child has pain because her time has come; but when her baby is born she forgets the anguish because of her joy that a child is born into the world. So with you: Now is your time of grief, but I will see you again and you will rejoice, and no one will take away your joy."[41]

The pain of labor is quickly forgotten when a new mother is holding her precious son or daughter in her arms. Joy and love overflow her heart to the point that not only has she forgotten the pain she endured, but she is more often than not willing to do it again to once again feel that joy.

Can you imagine a mother right in the middle of labor saying to the doctor, "That's it. I can't take the pain any longer. I knew the pain was going to be bad, but nobody said it would be this bad! I know having a baby would be a wonderful thing, a miracle even, but I am kinda done for tonight. I am gonna head on home, and I will see you later." *No!* Of course she wouldn't stop because her eyes are on the prize of the life she is bringing into the world.

Just like that mom, we can't stop either. God is using the pain in our lives during our waiting time as His way to birth many wonderful things in us and to bring unspeakable joy into our lives. He is birthing compassion and spiritual fruit in us for the achievement of eternal glory. Wow...eternal glory! I had given up on even attaining earthly glory, but God speaks of eternal glory. Compassion? Spiritual fruits? Eternal glory? What does that mean for us?

Pain's sorrow in our hearts yields something that nothing else can—compassion. It is only when you have hurt to the very core of who you are, to the point you are not sure if you can take another breath, that compassion for those hurting in similar ways is born. Your own heart breaks under the pain of heavy grief, but God sees the sorrow deepening your sympathy for those who need a champion in what is breaking their hearts.

Our waiting time also produces spiritual fruit. "Outwardly it may appear painful or even destructive, but inwardly its spiritual work produces blessings. Many of the richest blessings we have inherited are through the fruit of sorrow or pain. We should never forget that redemption, the world's greatest blessing, is the fruit of the world's greatest sorrow."[42]

Just as a gardener understands exactly where and when to prune his vineyards to get the very best fruit, so God prunes areas in our lives because He knows what we can become. It appears He is cutting everything away, and the pain of it is beyond what we think we can bear. But He sees our future, and He knows that our lives will be enriched, and the fruit we produce will be amazing.

Beyond compassion and spiritual fruit, God tells us that our pain has eternal significance. "For our light and momentary troubles are achieving for us an eternal glory that far outweighs them all."[43] Why do our lives have to be filled with so much pain? The answer is in the word "achieving," for our "momentary troubles are achieving" "an eternal glory." In God's just economy, there is a reward for every sorrow. In this life, sorrow produces that reward.

The reality is that God is not wasting the pain. He never wastes the pain in your life but often uses it to show us dreams bigger than we could never have dreamed up on our own. "In our greatest pain we need to lean heavily on God. He's using our weakness to do His work in and through us, building trust, so that His dream for each of our lives can become a reality."[44]

God doesn't want our pain to destroy us. He wants it to transform us. That means we have to trust Him and not let our emotions and the pain that we are feeling take us down the path of fear, doubt, resentment, and bitterness. When we trust Him, our hope is buoyed, and we find the strength to make it through another day.

In Psalm 30:5, we are reminded that "Weeping may stay for the night, but rejoicing comes in the morning."[45] Now obviously, if your pain has not lasted just one night but many nights, you are giving this verse *that* look. I know *that* look because that verse has received that same look from me a number of times. So, let's rethink this from an eternal perspective. In light of today, it feels like it will last its own eternity. In light of *eternity*, our pain and sorrow will only stay for what appears to be a night. That helps make things a bit clearer!

But the message to take away from this verse is that our pain will end. It will not last forever. We will rejoice once again in the blessings that God has bestowed in our lives. Remember, there is never a majestic mountain without a valley, and there is no birth without pain. Waiting for that beauty and joy is painful to the very core of who we are, but it's really the only thing worth truly waiting for.

Just like that new mom, our pain will fade to but a memory when the beauty of God's blessings rains down on us, leaving us with unimagined, inexpressible joy. We will have a reason to sing because the pain we are currently feeling will not compare to the joy that is coming. We just have to wait and fight on one day at a time.

The Suffering in Waiting

Suffering is defined as "the bearing of pain or distress."[46] We have no greater example than that of Job, an ordinary man who suffered extraordinary pain and distress in this life. Just as a refresher: Job experienced loss on a variety of levels, and he experienced it in a devastating fashion. His 500 yoke of oxen and 500 donkeys were all stolen by the Sabeans. His 7,000 sheep were completely burned up by a fire that fell from the sky. His 3,000 camels were stolen by the Chaldeans. And his seven sons and three daughters were all killed when the home of his eldest son was destroyed by a mighty wind.

And this all happened in a single day!

If that wasn't enough to literally crush Job's soul, and before the grief of all of these calamities even had a chance to take hold of his heart, Job's wife said to him, "Are you still maintaining your integrity? Curse God and die!"[47] Okay, so she is definitely not going to make the list for "Greatest Encourager" in the Bible!

Her hateful words were then followed by the words of Job's "so-called" friends—Eliphaz, Bildad, and Zophar. These "gentlemen" tried to offer what they thought were words of encouragement by way of judgment and condemnation. And Job's heart was wounded even more deeply.

After seven days of complete and total silence, Job broke his silence, and in Job 3:1-26, we see and feel the suffering of this broken man.

After this, Job opened his mouth and cursed the day of his birth. He said:

> "May the day of my birth perish,
> and the night that said, 'A boy is conceived!'
> That day—may it turn to darkness;
> may God above not care about it;
> may no light shine on it.
> May gloom and utter darkness claim it once more;
> may a cloud settle over it;
> may blackness overwhelm it.
> That night—may thick darkness seize it;
> may it not be included among the days of the year
> nor be entered in any of the months.
> May that night be barren;
> may no shout of joy be heard in it.
> May those who curse days curse that day,
> those who are ready to rouse Leviathan.
> May its morning stars become dark;

may it wait for daylight in vain
and not see the first rays of dawn,
for it did not shut the doors of the womb on me
to hide trouble from my eyes.
"Why did I not perish at birth,
and die as I came from the womb?
Why were there knees to receive me
and breasts that I might be nursed?
For now I would be lying down in peace;
I would be asleep and at rest
with kings and rulers of the earth,
who built for themselves places now lying in ruins,
with princes who had gold,
who filled their houses with silver.
Or why was I not hidden away in the ground like a stillborn child,
like an infant who never saw the light of day?
There the wicked cease from turmoil,
and there the weary are at rest.
Captives also enjoy their ease;
they no longer hear the slave driver's shout.
The small and the great are there,
and the slaves are freed from their owners.
"Why is light given to those in misery,
and life to the bitter of soul,
to those who long for death that does not come,
who search for it more than for hidden treasure,
who are filled with gladness
and rejoice when they reach the grave?
Why is life given to a man
whose way is hidden,
whom God has hedged in?
For sighing has become my daily food;

my groans pour out like water.
What I feared has come upon me;
what I dreaded has happened to me.
I have no peace, no quietness;
I have no rest, but only turmoil."[48]

Job's heart was so full of suffering that he cursed the very day of his birth. In subsequent chapters, he cried out to God and asked God why He was allowing this. What was the purpose in this incredible amount of suffering? Did God really care about him anymore?

As we wait and we suffer, we are sitting right where Job was. We are asking God those questions and many more. Perhaps the two questions that linger the longest in our minds are: why am I going through this suffering? And when will it end?

Unfortunately, Job did not get an answer to his question of why he was enduring this incredible amount of suffering, and sometimes we don't either. There are times when we are suffering that we simply must give up the why. Now, I don't say that easily. Saying I like to understand the why behind what is going on is a bit of an understatement. I *need* to understand the why. When I can understand the why, I can usually work through whatever situation I find myself in far more productively. But sometimes, God chooses not to reveals it to us. Instead, He simply asks us to give up the why and trust Him with all that is going on in and around us.

Although we may not have the why of our suffering in waiting revealed to us, there are five big picture things we can hold on to during this time:

1. Every heartache moves the heart of God.

2. Part of God's promised blessing to us may involve delay and suffering.

3. God can best use us when our will is bent to His, and that often involves being completely broken through suffering.

4. Being obedient and experiencing suffering is the highest form of faith.

5. We will be rewarded for obedience during our suffering.

So, let's dig into these points together, one by one. First of all, every heartache we experience moves the heart of God. In Psalm 56:8, David tells us just how intimately aware of our suffering God is as he says, "You keep track of all my sorrows. You have collected all my tears in your bottle. You have recorded each one in your book."[49] In my own period of waiting, I know God must have pulled out a *very big* bottle for the many, many tears I cried. Although I am typically not a regular crier, I have undoubtedly met my lifetime quota of tears during that very difficult season of my life!

What an amazing picture of God's love for us. He doesn't just keep track of the biggest sorrows in our life that have smashed our hearts to smithereens. He keeps track of *all* our sorrows. And He has collected *all* our tears. Every single tear I cried, He caught. Every single tear that has trickled down your cheeks, He collected. He even caught those tears we cried into our pillows when we were alone at night, feeling absolutely hopeless. He has been there when we cried so hard we could not shed another tear. We are that precious to Him.

We are so precious to Him that He wants to give us all the good things He can in this life. Romans 8:32 reminds us, " He who did not spare his own Son, but gave Him up for us all — how will He not also, along with Him, graciously give us all things?"[50] God gave the life of His very own Son so that we might have eternal life. Just think of what that cost Him. It cost Him everything, and that is how much He loves us. If He was willing to do that, just imagine what more He wants to give us in our lives today...sometimes they just come with the price tag of waiting.

To our second point, as much as our tears and sorrows move the heart of God, we can be certain that delay and suffering are often an integral part of His promised blessing to us. As we look at Abraham's life, God's promise of a son was followed by what seemed to be an unending delay and, therefore, great suffering as his wife went from being fertile to barren. In Joseph's life, his God-given dream was followed by suffering in the form of slavery, false accusations, and false imprisonment.

But in both cases, God's promises stood. Abraham had a miracle in his son Isaac, as he was born well past Sarah's childbearing years. Joseph's dreams came true to the very last detail, and God honored His promise as Joseph became the second most powerful man in the land of Egypt. Through all the trying years these men waited and suffered, God's promises stood and were fulfilled at the proper time. Their faith was answered in a resounding way.

Our third point is a tough one to hear in that God can best use us when our will is bent to His, and that often involves being completely broken through suffering. Why?

> The best things in life are the result of being wounded. Wheat must be crushed before becoming bread, and incense must be burned by fire before its fragrance is set free. The earth must be broken with a sharp plow before being ready to receive the seed. And it is a broken heart that pleases God. Yes, the sweetest joys of life are the fruits of sorrow. Human nature seems to need suffering to make it fit to be a blessing to the world.[51]

Our very human nature is transformed, by God's grace, through suffering. God uses suffering to remove from us a selfish heart of stone and replaces it with a giving heart of love for others and strength of character that is unmatched. You see, "It is from suffering that the strongest souls ever known have emerged; the world's greatest display of character is seen in those who exhibit the scars of sorrow; the martyrs of the ages have worn their coronation robes that have glistened with fire, yet through their tears and sorrow have seen the gates of heaven."[52] Joseph suffered more than any of Jacob's other sons, but it led him into a position and a food ministry that impacted entire nations.

Now, this may be of little consolation to us as we struggle to get through a day with our hearts in one piece. But there are truly some areas of Christian growth and maturity that can only be reached through the doorway of tremendous suffering. The source of learning to help others and deepening our compassion and empathy for those who are suffering often comes only as being in the classroom of suffering.

And if we are honest with ourselves, I know we will find that the people in our lives we regularly turn to for advice and comfort are the ones who have been through tremendous trials and suffering. There is a depth to these people that seems to go on and on...touching our hearts and souls because we know that they literally feel what we are going through.

They feel what we are going through because they have been there themselves in one way or another.

We, too, will gain this kind of depth as we let God use our waiting and our suffering to chisel out any flaws and deformities in our cavernous characters that need to be carved out. In many cases, we find that sorrow reveals unknown depths of our souls. And sorrow is God's tool to plow the depths of our soul to even deeper levels in order that there will be a richer harvest.

> If humankind were still in a glorified state, having never fallen, then the strong floods of the divine joy would be the force God would use to reveal our soul's capacities. But in a fallen world, sorrow, yet with despair removed, is the power chosen to reveal us to ourselves. Accordingly, it is sorrow that causes us to take the time to think deeply and seriously.[53]

Our fourth point is that being obedient and experiencing suffering is the highest form of faith. When God calls us into a period of waiting, and that waiting includes suffering in a way we have never suffered before, then great faith is being obedient no matter how much it hurts. Great faith is exhibited in our willingness to bear the suffering, endure the suffering, and fight through the suffering with the faith that God has a purpose in it all.

Why is suffering such a key part of this equation of faith? Suffering is a key part of the faith equation because it conforms us to the likeness of Christ. "Waiting on God and abiding in His will is to know Him through 'participation in his sufferings'[54] and 'to be conformed to the image of his Son.[55] '"[56] Therefore, we need to "rejoice inasmuch as [we] participate in the sufferings of Christ, so that [we] may be overjoyed when his glory is revealed."[57]

The sufferings of Christ were beyond intense—physically, emotionally, and spiritually. In terms of His physical suffering, Isaiah 52:14 reveals that when He made His way to the site of His crucifixion, Jesus' "appearance was so disfigured beyond that of any human being and His form marred beyond human likeness."[58] He had been flogged, a crown of thorns smashed into His head, and stones were thrown at Him. By the end of the day, nails had been driven into His hands and feet, and His side was pierced by a spear. His death was brutal, and the physical suffering beyond anything we can fathom today.

His emotional suffering was equally as difficult because Jesus knew what was to come. He knew the physical torture that He would endure, and so, He and the disciples went to the Garden of Gethsemane to pray before Judas' betrayal. As they arrived in Gethsemane, Jesus was deeply troubled and full of sorrow. "Then He said to them, 'My soul is overwhelmed with sorrow to the point of death.'"[59]

"Going a little farther, He fell with His face to the ground and prayed, 'My Father, if it is possible, may this cup be taken from Me. Yet not as I will, but as you will.'"[60] "He went away a second time and prayed, 'My Father, if it is not possible for this cup to be taken away unless I drink it, may your will be done.'"[61] He then "went away once more and prayed the third time, saying the same thing."[62]

Just a quick interlude here, the times between His prayers, Jesus was going back to check on His disciples who had fallen asleep in the Garden. In the midst of facing the single most agonizing time of His life, His concern was on His followers. His mind was on the men He so dearly loved.

Three times Jesus prayed that the Lord would take the cup of suffering from Him. Luke 22:44 says that He was in such anguish as He prayed these prayers that "His sweat was like drops of blood falling to the ground."[63] And more of His blood fell that day, as we know that the cup of suffering was not removed. Jesus went on to do the will of the Father by laying His life down as the payment for our sins.

As horrendous as His physical and emotional suffering was, nothing compared to the spiritual suffering He experienced. Second Corinthians 5:21 says, "God made Him who had no sin to be sin for us, so that in Him we might become the righteousness of God."[64] Jesus bore the weight of the sins of the entire world—past, present, and future—as He hung on the cross. The weight of this sin caused Him to cry out as He hung on the cross, "My God, my God, why have you forsaken Me?"[65] At this moment in time, Jesus felt completely separated from God as if God had turned His back on His own Son, who had obediently done as His Father willed.

Hebrews 2:10 says, "In bringing many sons and daughters to glory, it was fitting that God, for whom and through whom everything exists, should make the pioneer of their salvation perfect through what He suffered."[66] Jesus was already perfect, but He fulfilled the perfect plan of salvation through what He obediently suffered through. It was God's plan all along. The path to glory was the path of obedience and suffering.

And it was through His suffering that Jesus identifies with our suffering. He knows what waiting requires, and He knows the price of obedience. It cost Him His very life. But He also knows that true sympathy for another person's broken heart often comes at the price of our own broken heart through the same or similar afflictions. The school of suffering graduates exceptional scholars of sympathy that can go on to show Christ's love in magnificent ways.

Unfortunately, there is only one way to get there...the hard way. The development of our character occurs not through luxurious living but through suffering. And the world remembers people of great character.

Our fifth and final point is that we will be rewarded for obedience during our suffering. Psalm 126:5 says, "Those who sow with tears will reap with songs of joy."[67] Psalm 84:11 tells us, "For the LORD God is a sun and shield; The LORD gives grace and glory; No good thing does He withhold from those who walk uprightly."[68]

We see this promise lived out in the life of Job. When the time of his suffering came to an end,

> The LORD blessed the latter part of Job's life more than the former part. He had fourteen thousand sheep, six thousand camels, a thousand yoke of oxen, and a thousand donkeys. And he also had seven sons and three daughters. The first daughter he named Jemimah, the second Keziah, and the third Keren-Happuch. Nowhere in all the land were there found women as beautiful as Job's daughters, and their father granted them an inheritance along with their brothers. After this, Job lived a hundred and forty years; he saw his children and their children to the fourth generation. And so, Job died, an old man and full of years.[69]

All that Job had been through could have turned him angry and resentful towards God, but instead, he was humbled before the God of the universe. In obedience, he refused to curse God but rather thanked him for the life that he had been given. In turn, God blessed Job with double the cattle he had before his trials began, seven more sons and three more daughters. All that was taken was replaced and with a richer blessing attached.

As hard as our period of suffering is—and believe me, I know just how hard it is as many days have found me with my face down in the carpet, just weeping, praying, and asking for God's mercy to lift this time of waiting—the rewards will be worth the wait. Tribulation opens the door to triumph, and God is with us each step of the way until the door is blown open. We are never out of His view, no matter how black the darkness is around us. He is there, cheering us on until we faithfully cross the finish line, and He blesses us beyond our imagination.

The Trial of Waiting

The trial of waiting seems to place us smack dab in the middle of trouble. Often, when we walk through these times of trouble, we begin to feel we are past the point of being delivered. This is when God reminds us of His precious promise, "Though I walk in the midst of trouble, You preserve my life."[70]

God's answer may seem forever in coming, especially as we walk in the "midst of trouble." But if we step back for even just the briefest of seconds, we may just see God's protection all around us. Instead of being in the center of trouble, we are in the eye of the storm—the safest place to be. You see, faith sees God through the eye of the storm.

Our trials of waiting are growing our faith in incredible ways. Our trials have a way of bringing us to the end of ourselves, and this is where the secret of God's complete sufficiency is revealed. It is through the trials that we come face to face with our own inadequacy and frailty—as we truly are jars of clay—in the light of His all-sufficient strength and grace. As 2 Corinthians 4:7 says, "We have this treasure in jars of clay to show that this all surpassing power is from God and not from us."[71]

It is then that we come to lean on the Lord for longer periods of time and with more of our heart, soul, and mind. God knows that many times in our lives, the strong and constant pressure of a trial is the only way we will come to lean completely on Him. As we lean on Him, we will find that He can bear all our weight for as long as we need to place it on Him.

The beauty of the trials that we face, even in our waiting, is that they are sent to make us, not break us. A direct blow to our outer person can be an amazing blessing in terms of how it builds our inner person—particularly our faith. First Peter 1:6-7 says, "In all this you greatly rejoice, though now for a little while you may have had to suffer grief in all kinds of trials. These have come so that the proven genuineness of your faith—of greater worth than gold, which perishes even though refined by fire—may result in praise, glory and honor when Jesus Christ is revealed."[72] Our trials are sent to test, refine, and burn away all but the purest aspects of our faith.

The refining of our faith is much like the process of refining fine china.

The world's finest china is fired in ovens at least three times, and some many more. Dresden china is always fired three times. Why is it forced to endure such intense heat? Shouldn't once or twice be enough? No, it is necessary to fire the china three times so the gold, crimson, and other colors are brighter, more beautiful, and permanently attached.

We are fashioned after the same principle. The human trials of life are burned into us numerous times, and through God's grace, beautiful colors are formed in us and made to shine forever.[73]

Sometimes in the heat of the fire of our trials, the pain is unbearable. Instead of bringing forth beautiful colors, we feel more like the fire is shattering us into a million jagged pieces. But it is precisely in that very heat that our faith will be perfected, especially if even under the pain we can continue to praise God for His goodness and love that has brought this trial into our lives in the first place.

So, how do we turn our trial into a triumph in our lives? Warren Wiersbe says,

If we are going to turn trials into triumphs, we must obey four imperatives: count (James 1:2), know (James 1:3), let (James 1:4, 9-11), and ask (James 1:5-8). Or, to put it another way, there are four essentials for victory in trials: a joyful attitude, an understanding mind, a surrendered will, and a heart that wants to believe.[74]

The first imperative is to have a joyful attitude. In John 16:33, we are told, "I have told you these things, so that in me you may have peace. In this world you will have trouble. But take heart! I have overcome the world." The Bible tells us in no uncertain terms we are going to have trouble and trials. But James 1:2 encourages us in the midst of these trials by saying, "Consider it pure joy, my brothers and sisters, whenever you face trials of many kinds."[75] "Outlook determines outcome; to end with joy, begin with joy."[76] But how can we possibly rejoice in the midst of a trial when our hearts are breaking?

That's where we need to dive into the second imperative. We must have an understanding mind. The reality of our trials is that they work for us, not against us. "God always tests us to bring out the best; Satan tempts us to bring out the worst."[77]

Part of that "best" is our willingness to persevere. As James 1:3-4 tells us, "the testing of your faith produces perseverance. Let perseverance finish its work so that you may be mature and complete, not lacking anything."[78] Perseverance is key to the Lord maturing us spiritually because it is our willingness to keep going even when things are at their worst. As Romans 5:3-4 tells us, "Not only so, but we also glory in our sufferings, because we know that suffering produces perseverance; perseverance, character; and character, hope."[79]

The only way the Lord can develop patience and character in our lives is through trials. Endurance cannot be attained by reading a book (even this one), listening to a sermon, or even praying a prayer. We must go through the difficulties of life, trust God, and obey Him. The result will be patience and character. Knowing this, we can face trials joyfully. We know what trials will do in us and for us, and we know that the end result will bring glory to God.[80]

God wants to mature us and grow our patience because it is the key to every other blessing. Now I am not talking about patience in the sense of passively accepting our circumstances. Biblical patience is far from passive. "It is a courageous perseverance in the face of suffering and difficulty."[81] As difficult as it is, when we learn to wait on the Lord, then God can do great things for us.

All of this leads us to our third imperative—a surrendered will. "God cannot build our character without our cooperation."[82] There are three works involved in the complete Christian life.

First, there is the work God does *for us*, which is salvation. Jesus Christ completed this work on the cross. If we trust Him, He will save us. Second, there is the work God does *in us*: "For we are His workmanship." This work is known as sanctification: God builds our character and we become more like Jesus Christ, "conformed to the image of his Son."[83] The third work is what God does *through us*—service. We are "created in Christ Jesus unto good works."[84]

God builds character before He calls to service. He must work in us before He can work through us. God spent twenty-five years working in Abraham before He could give him his promised son. God worked thirteen years in Joseph's life, putting him into "various testings" before He could put him on the throne of Egypt. He spent eighty years preparing Moses for forty years of service. Our Lord took three years training His disciples, building their character.[85]

Character building takes time, and that is part of the reason for our waiting. This leads us to the final imperative—a believing heart. James 1:5-8 says,

> If any of you lacks wisdom, you should ask God, who gives generously to all without finding fault, and it will be given to you. But when you ask, you must believe and not doubt, because the one who doubts is like a wave of the sea, blown and tossed by the wind. That person should not expect to receive anything from the Lord. Such a person is double-minded and unstable in all they do.[86]

As we are facing these difficult trials in our lives, knowing God is using them to mature us, we need to ask Him for wisdom. We want to make sure we are learning what we need to in these circumstances and that no lesson goes unlearned before the trial ends. The Lord knows we don't want to go through a similar trial again to re-learn a lesson we already had the chance to learn once!

When we follow these four imperatives, we can rejoice in the trials that we face. Yes, it is possible that the heat of my own trials has literally fried my brain for me to say that, but not regarding this point. Every trial that hits us is *never* by chance but by God's divine direction. Every trial has a special mission by which God has purposed to accomplish something very specific in our lives. As 2 Corinthians 4:16-18 reminds us, "Therefore we do not lose heart. Though outwardly we are wasting away, yet inwardly we are being renewed day by day. For our light and momentary troubles are achieving for us an eternal glory that far outweighs them all. So we fix our eyes not on what is seen, but on what is unseen, since what is seen is temporary, but what is unseen is eternal."[87]

We may not know why He sent the trial or exactly what He wants to accomplish. But we can continue to "believe that out of the fire will arise something more worthy of praise to Him than we had ever experienced."[88] We must win the victory in the fire.

In fact, the very trial that has come into our lives may put us on the path to our destiny. Often, our detours or what we believe to be detours are steering us in the direction we were meant to go all along. Without these trials, we would not get where God wants us to go.

Part of getting where God wants us to go involves our trials because, without a doubt, we know that our trials are the path to our crowns. James 1:12 says, "Blessed is the one who perseveres under trial because, having stood the test, that person will receive the crown of life that the Lord has promised to those who love Him."[89] The very hardships we are enduring today have been given to us by our loving Heavenly Father for the express purpose of enabling us to win our crowns.

> Rise today to face the circumstances in which the providence of God has placed you. Your crown of glory is hidden in the heart of these things—the hardships and trials pressing in on you this very hour, week, and month of your life. Yet the most difficult things are not those seen and known by the world but those deep within your soul, unseen and unknown by anyone except Jesus. It is in this secret place that you experience a little trial that you would never dare to mention to anyone else and that is more difficult for you to bear than martyrdom.[90]

Although difficult to bear, thankfully, our gracious God never gives us a trial that we cannot withstand. So, the trial that we are currently in is one that He knows we can make it through. He knows our strength, and He measures it to the last drop. As we struggle day by day to make it through our trial of waiting, we just need to remember: no trial has ever been given to anyone that was greater than his or her strength to endure it through God's power.

On those days, we forget that, and it appears our trial will end in certain defeat, it is wonderful to remind ourselves that God has a track record of winning His greatest victories through apparent defeat. There may even be times in our waiting that Satan seems to be winning the battle, but only because God allows it. Then in the eleventh hour, God comes in, overthrows the enemy's work, and wins the war. "Consequently, He gives us a much greater victory than we would have known had He not allowed the enemy seemingly to triumph in the first place."[91] So do not acknowledge defeat. Continue to claim faith in Him who has made us "more than conquerors,"[92]   and a glorious victory will soon be seen. "Defeat may serve as well as victory to shake the soul and let the glory out."[93]

Whether we are facing defeat or victory, there is one thing we can know for sure about our trials...eventually they will come to an end. Every trial has an ending. Every storm will pass.

There is a limit to our affliction, and God knows that limit. He sends the trial we face, and then He removes it when it is time, and His purpose has been fully accomplished. He Himself said in Nahum 1:12, "Although I have afflicted you...I will afflict you no more."[94] "Weeping may stay for the night, but rejoicing comes in the morning."[95]

After what seems like an eternity, the fire will die down, and just like the china with its vibrant colors on display, we will display God's glory in our spiritual vibrancy. Our trial of waiting will come to an end. The fire will have been hotter at times than we believed we could survive, and the pain unbearable. But God has His hand on the thermostat, and He knows just when the firing process has achieved all it was intended to achieve.

Great faith must first endure great trials. "God's greatest gifts come through great pain."[96] In the meantime, we can climb closer to God on that path of pain, knowing that God walks with us in the midst of our trials and it's in the trials of the valleys that we grow.

Weariness, Brokenness, and God's Grace

Weariness

In the darkness, despair, pain, suffering, and trials of waiting, we often find ourselves weary in both heart and spirit. Our hearts grow weary in the waiting, especially when the painful situations last for long periods of time. We pray and pray, but God doesn't seem to be listening. We wait and wait, but nothing seems to be happening. Our will to keep on fighting begins to wane, and our spirit begins to grow weak.

We see the psalmist experiencing that same weariness as he writes, "My soul is weary with sorrow; strengthen me according to your word."[97] "I am worn out calling for help; my throat is parched. My eyes fail, looking for God to help me."[98] "My eyes fail, looking for your promise; I say, 'When will you comfort me?'"[99]

This is the time Satan does his best to fill our minds with doubt and unbelief about God's love, faithfulness, and goodness. Satan's goal is to bring enough distrust into our minds that we simply stop waiting, take the situation into our own hands, and make the wrong decisions. In fact, in the Screwtape Letters by C. S. Lewis, one demon says to the other, "The fun is to make the man yield just when (had he but known it) relief was almost in sight."[100]

Brokenness

Not only does waiting bring weariness in heart and spirit, but it also reveals brokenness in our lives. In my time of waiting, my brokenness has shown itself in my impatience, spiritual immaturity, selfishness, and, yes, at times, unbelief in God's ability to work out my situation. My own time of waiting gave me far more time than I would have liked to have to examine my own thoughts...and wow... some of them were just doozies. Some even left me saying, "Did that really come out of my head? (Or even worse, my mouth!) Lord, You have *so* much work to do!"

That kind of brokenness reveals our desperate need for God's grace to heal and restore us so we can become all that He intends us to be. It is then that we can see there is beauty in our brokenness, as we bring all our broken pieces to God, and He proceeds to mend our broken hearts and dreams, for He is waiting to use something far more powerful than superglue to put us back together. He is waiting to use His Love.

And He wants us to bring our brokenness and all the shattered pieces of our lives to Him, so He can make us whole once again. You see, He has all the blueprints of our lives because He created us. He knows where works need to be done. He knows where additions have been made and where renovations need to occur. He knows where the secret hideaways are that no one else knows about. At times, He may need to even knock down a wall or two or open some of the secret hideaways to rebuild something far more beautiful, strong, and stable in its place.

Believe me when I say that this is not easy and having a wall or two knocked down in our lives often leaves us feeling pummeled. I get it. Sometimes I feel like God has leveled my whole house instead of just a few walls. But I believe out of brokenness can come good. I believe that relationships can be restored, emotions stabilized, minds healed, and character deepened. I believe that our brokenness can be a time where miracles happen. And the most miraculous thing that can occur is our getting a deeper understanding of God's grace.

God's Grace

I heard a definition of God's sustaining grace as this: "Sustaining grace—a specific, timely infusion of God's strength in a Christ-follower, to allow her to find hope and endurance" (source unknown). I absolutely loved that definition, but I wanted to add something to it. My definition would go a little something like this: "Sustaining grace—a specific, timely infusion of God's strength in a Christ-follower, to allow her to find hope and endurance in her process of spiritual maturity."

Let's break down this definition a bit. First of all, God's grace, especially in our time of waiting, is timely. Hebrews 4:16 says, "Let us then approach God's throne of grace with confidence, so that we may receive mercy and find grace to help us in our time of need."[101] We aren't directed to ask for God's sustaining grace before our time of need or after our time of need as we wait...but in our time of need. Right at the moment when we need it the most, God is directing us to ask for His sustaining grace.

Secondly, God's grace is there to strengthen us. When we are weary and broken in our waiting, God says in 2 Corinthians 12:9, "'My grace is sufficient for you, for my power is made perfect in weakness.' Therefore I will boast all the more gladly about my weaknesses, so that Christ's power may rest on me."[102] God puts trials in our lives that we simply cannot handle on our own strength so that we come to depend on Him and watch the mightiness of His strength on display.

Lastly, God's sustaining grace is there to help us in our process of spiritual maturity. God's grace allows us to weather the most difficult times of waiting in our lives without losing all hope. And He will allow specific trials in our lives to help shape and mature us. Recall James 1:2-4, "Consider it pure joy, my brothers and sisters, whenever you face trials of many kinds, because you know that the testing of your faith produces perseverance. Let perseverance finish its work so that you may be mature and complete, not lacking anything."[103]

Maturity and completeness come with a price, and for us, that price is a period of waiting. We can turn off the pain and suffering in our lives, but when we do that, we also turn off the pleasure, joy, and the growth that we will get through the process. Galatians 6:9 is reassuring as it says, "Let us not become weary in doing good, for at the proper time we will reap a harvest if we do not give up."[104] We will reap the harvest of spiritual maturity if we hold on to God's timely and strengthening sustaining grace as we patiently wait. Don't grow weary!

Chapter 3

Why God Makes Us Wait

Why Do We Have to Wait?

Why do we have to wait? I believe that is the million-dollar question, and I believe the million-dollar answers are found in the pages of Scripture. We have to wait for four very important reasons:

1. God is arranging the circumstances.
2. God is refining us like gold.
3. God is preparing us for what He has in store for us.
4. God is bringing us into true intimacy with Himself.

Let's look at each one of these four points and understand exactly what they mean for us in a very practical sense.

God is Arranging the Circumstances

Point one: we must wait because God is arranging the circumstances. In Scripture, we see repeatedly how God made a promise to someone and then made that person wait for the fruition of that promise as He arranged the circumstances. David is a perfect example as he was crowned King of Israel at a very young age. He had to wait over twenty years to eventually claim the throne, and the waiting was not punctuated by a time of luxury and ease. For much of it, King Saul, the reigning King of Israel, was so threatened by David that he hunted David down like an animal, fully intending to kill him. God, however, had His hand on David, and Saul's advances were thwarted.

There were also times during this period where David could have easily taken Saul's life and ended not only his wait for the throne but, more importantly, put to rest the daily fear he felt for his life.

But David listened intently to the Lord's direction and continued to wait patiently for God to remove Saul from the throne in His own way and in His own time. In fact, Saul and his army were eventually defeated by the Philistines, resulting in Saul taking his own life. Instead of taking matters into his own hands, he waited while God worked behind the scenes to mature him as a leader and clear the path to the throne in a way that prevented Saul's blood from being on his hands.

Just as with David, God will continue to give us wisdom and direction when we seek Him, often using our circumstances to guide us. Horace Bushnell writes,

> One moment, our way may seem totally blocked, but then suddenly some seemingly trivial incident occurs, appearing as nothing to others but speaking volumes to the keen eye of faith. And sometimes, these events are repeated in various ways in response to our prayers. They certainly are not haphazard results of chance but are God opening up the way we should walk by directing our circumstances. And they begin to multiply as we advance toward our goal, just as the lights of a city seem to increase as we speed toward it while traveling at night.[105]

If you go to God for guidance, He will guide you. What He will do, if you will trust Him and go cheerfully ahead when He shows you the way, is to guide you still farther.

Just remember, God is arranging the circumstances.

God is Refining Us Like Gold

Point two: God is refining us like gold. Waiting is not just about what we get at the end of the wait, but about whom we are becoming as we wait. Like gold, we are being refined. In fact, the Bible even speaks of the process of our refinement using the analogy of gold. First Peter 1:6-7 says, "In all this you greatly rejoice, though now for a little while you may have had to suffer grief in all kinds of trials. These have come so that the proven genuineness of your faith—of greater worth than gold, which perishes even though refined by fire—may result in praise, glory and honor when Jesus Christ is revealed."[106] Malachi 3:3 reiterated this point by saying, "He will sit as a refiner and purifier of silver."[107]

Refining with flame is one of the oldest methods of refining metals. Mentioned even in the Bible, refining by fire is the preferable method for larger quantities of gold. In ancient times, this form of refining involved a craftsman sitting next to a hot fire with molten gold in a crucible being stirred and skimmed to remove the impurities or dross that rose to the top of the molten metal. With flames reaching temperatures in excess of 1000 degrees Celsius, this job was a dangerous occupation for the gold refiner. The tradition remains largely untouched today with the exception of a few advancements in safety and precision.[108]

Our Father, who seeks to perfect us, knows the value of the refiner's fire. It is with the most precious metals that a metallurgist takes the greatest care. He or she subjects the precious metal to a hot fire to release the impurities. The result is a perfectly pure metal that is ready to take a new shape.

Just as a good refiner would never leave the crucible, God will sit down by it so the fire will not become even one degree too hot and permanently damage the metal. God's goal is to only leave us in the fire long enough to skim the impurities out of our lives so that we shine brighter and brighter. And as soon as He skims the last bit of impurity from the surface and sees His face reflected in the pure metal, He extinguishes the fire.

Can't you just see God sitting at a crucible, next to a thousand-degree fire, removing our impurities as they bubble up to the surface? I can! I can see God stirring the gold of my heart and watching as all the things I would like to keep hidden rise to the top:

- My doubts in His promises
- My fears
- My desire to be in control (any semblance of control most days)
- My lack of trust
- My rebellious nature
- My pride
- My selfish desires.

Here is what is amazing: He sees them all as they rise to the surface, and rather than throwing out my whole pot of gold, He skims these impurities off the surface as if they never existed. Even when we don't see it in ourselves, He sees gold in our hearts, and He is intent on refining that gold. And He would not spend the time refining us if He didn't have a beautiful purpose behind it.

The refinement and purification of our hearts require us, just like gold, to be in the crucible. Now, this is what just blows me away. The word "crucible" has two meanings:

1. "A ceramic or metal container in which metals or other substances may be melted or subjected to very high temperatures.
2. "A place or occasion of severe test or trial."[109]

Just like gold in its metal container is subjected to extremely high temperatures, so are we in our trials subjected to enormous pain. Pulling out our impurities is not an easy process because many of them are deeply ingrained. At least mine are! So, the fire must continue to burn until the impurities have been pulled out. The most difficult part of being kept in the crucible is the time. We could easily endure a short firing up and cooling down, but when the fire of our trials continues to burn on and on, our hearts lose strength.

Joseph endured a very long, difficult series of trials, including enslavement, servitude, false accusation, and imprisonment. God used that series of trials to burn into the depths of Joseph's being the lessons he would need to lead the nation of Egypt through one of the most difficult times it faced in its history. And when the lessons had been learned, and God knew Joseph's character was ready for the challenge soon to come, the flame was put out.

Thankfully, we, too, can trust God that explicitly. We can trust God to sit patiently watching the fire so that we will not be kept in our crucible of waiting one second longer than is necessary to accomplish His purposes. We can trust that God will stop the fire the moment He can see His own image glowing in the gold of our hearts. And like Job, we too can say, "But He knows the way that I take; when He has tested me, I will come forth as gold."[110]

As God has tested me and used the fire to refine me, I have watched the changes occurring in my own life. Others might have seen me as a woman "having it all together," while I often saw myself and certain aspects of my life as a "perfect disaster." I have watched God use my own crucible to transform me from a woman who did her Bible study out of obligation to one who wakes up every morning and dives into her devotionals before her feet hit the bedroom floor. I even use a flashlight, so I literally don't have to get out of bed until my devotionals are done. I have watched God transform me from a woman who would pray every now and then to one who is a pray warrior praying without ceasing for the things God lays on my heart. And I have watched God grab a hold of my heart so that the most important thing in my life was my relationship with Him. Now I pray that like Job, I can say: when God has tested me, I will come out as gold.

An unknown poet expressed the depths of God's work in and through us in this way:

When God wants to drill a man,
And thrill a man,
And skill a man;

When God wants to mold a man
To play the noblest part,
Then He yearns with all his heart
To create so great and bold a man
That all the world shall be amazed,
Watch His methods, watch His ways—
How He ruthlessly perfects
Whom he royally elects.
How He hammers him and hurts him,
And with mighty blows, converts him
Into trial shapes of clay
Which only God understands.
While his tortured heart is crying,
And he lifts beseeching hands.
How he bends but never breaks
When his good He undertakes.
How He uses Whom He chooses,
And with every purpose, fuses him,
By every act, induces him
To try His splendor out.
God knows what he's about.[111]

God is Preparing Us for What He Has in Store for Us

Point three: God is preparing us for what He has in store for us. While we patiently wait on God, He's diligently working behind the scenes, and He's preparing us for His answers to our prayers. It happened just this way in the lives of Abraham, Moses, and Joseph. They were given promises, those promises were delayed, and it was only through the patient discipline of waiting that they were then equipped for the work to which God had called them.

David followed a similar path. "The Lord had to force David, through the discipline of many long and painful years, to learn of the almighty power and faithfulness of his God. Through those difficult years, he also grew in his knowledge of faith and godliness, which were indispensable principles of his glorious career as the king of Israel."[112]

Just as He did with David, God is growing our faith and our character in this time of waiting. Unfortunately, faith is rarely, if ever, grown in any other place than overwhelming and exhausting circumstances and during times that seem to simply stand still. The development of a deep, Christ-like character cannot be hurried. Just like physical growth, spiritual growth takes time, discipline, and yes, even times of waiting.

In today's culture, we are obsessed with speed in everything we do. How much quicker can we do our daily tasks? How much faster can we make our meals? How much time can we shave off our commute to work? (Oh wait! Maybe that's just me thinking my commute to work is actually a local Nascar event.) But God is far more interested in strength and stability than speed. Real maturity is gradual. Genuine growth takes time.

Although God could instantly transform us, He has chosen to develop us little by little so that we would not be completely overwhelmed with all that is about to hit us. Because you see, genuine growth and transformation require real change, and real change often means some pain along the way. "There is no growth without change; there is no change without fear or loss; and there is no loss without pain."[113]

If you have surrendered yourself to Christ, your present circumstances that seem to be pressing so hard against you are the perfect tool in the Father's hands to chisel you into shape for eternity. So, trust Him and never push away the instrument He is using, or you will miss the result of His work in your life.[114]

The reality of our waiting is that God wouldn't have us waiting here if there weren't something worth waiting for. As a friend of mine said, "Quality takes time." The quality we are waiting for takes time. The quality of God's work in us takes time. So, when it feels grueling to wait, when the longing of your heart does not subside, and when the whole trial seems unendurable, know that God has something wonderful in store for you. At the appointed time, our waiting will come to an end, and we will rise up and be equal to all God has prepared us for.

God is Bringing Us into True Intimacy with Himself

Point four: God is bringing us into true intimacy with Himself. The reality is that God wants a relationship with us more than anything else in this entire universe. He wanted it so much that He sacrificed His own Son on a cross so that He could spend eternity with us if we are willing to accept Him as our Lord and Savior.

And God knows exactly what we will need to go through to bring us into closeness with Him. "Our capacity for knowing God is enlarged when we are brought by Him into circumstances that cause us to exercise our faith."[115] For you and me, this period of waiting may be exactly what God is using to bring us closer to Him.

You see, during our waiting, God is bringing us to a place where our typical distractions are removed. It is a place where we often feel in limbo, and therefore, it is the place where God has our fullest attention. It is a perfect place for one on one time with God so that He can reveal things about Himself and help us to see things about ourselves that we may simply not have previously been able to see (or, quite honestly, ever wanted to see).

It is in this waiting place, where we often feel helpless and hopeless, that God will help us see that He is all we need. We lean longer and harder on God than we ever have in our previous circumstances, and we find that He can take the full weight of all our burdens and far more. "And nothing but the great trials and dangers we have experienced would ever have led some of us to know Him as we do, to trust Him as we have, and to draw from Him the great measure of His grace so indispensable during our times of greatest need."[116]

Our situation may look hopeless, but hopelessness is where God can show Himself far more powerfully in our lives. When we wait on God to reveal His will, we find that the true treasure is that oftentimes He reveals Himself to us. So, when our hearts and minds cry out to be released from our waiting time, let us remember that when we can't trace His hand, we can trust His heart.

God Has to Take the Egypt Out

Another potential answer to the "Why?" behind our waiting may simply be found in the statement "God has to take Egypt out." Let's look at what that means.

After hundreds of years spent in Egyptian captivity, God called Moses to lead His people, the Israelites, to the Promised Land of Canaan. As they grew closer to Canaan, God called Moses to send some men to explore the land and provide a report back. After forty days, they returned and, with fear in their hearts, stated, "We went into the land to which you sent us, and it does flow with milk and honey! But the people who live there are powerful, and the cities are fortified and very large."[117] "We can't attack those people; they are stronger than we are."[118]

To make matters worse, "All the Israelites grumbled against Moses and Aaron, and the whole assembly said to them, 'If only we had died in Egypt! Or in this wilderness! Why is the LORD bringing us to this land only to let us fall by the sword? Our wives and children will be taken as plunder. Wouldn't it be better for us to go back to Egypt?' And they said to each other, 'We should choose a leader and go back to Egypt.'"[119]

So, after all, God had done—all the miracles, all the provisions, all the protection—the Israelites were ready to hightail it back to Egypt with the first sign of trouble. Well, this did not sit well with God.

"The LORD said to Moses, 'How long will these people treat Me with contempt? How long will they refuse to believe in Me, despite all the signs I have performed among them? I will strike them down with a plague and destroy them, but I will make you into a nation greater and stronger than they.'"[120]

Moses begged and pleaded for the lives of the Israelites to be spared, and God had mercy. But there were still consequences. In Numbers 14:34-35, God declares their punishment as this: "For forty years—one year for each of the forty days you explored the land—you will suffer for your sins and know what it is like to have Me against you. I, the LORD, have spoken, and I will surely do these things to this whole wicked community, which has banded together against Me. They will meet their end in this wilderness; here they will die."[121]

What could have been a forty-day journey to the Promised Land ended up being a forty-year punishment. So why did God do that? He did that because He had already gotten His children out of Egypt, but now He had to take Egypt out of His children.

The bottom line is that they were not prepared for what He had in store for them in Canaan. Their hearts, when things got rough, went immediately back to the place of their captivity—longing for what they had so badly wanted to leave. When pressed, they quickly forgot the pain they had endured there. And so, God gave them a forty-year journey to get Egypt completely out of their systems. I don't know about you, but if looking back over my shoulder at what should have remained in my past cost me forty years of wandering around in the wilderness, I would never, ever look back again.

Our waiting period may be the only way God can keep us from looking back at our "Egypt." Our waiting period may be the cornerstone of our own Exodus story...leaving behind the old and heading into the land full of God's promises for us. So rather than lament about where we are, we need to thank the Lord for loving us enough to get all the Egypt out.

His Perfect Plan

God has very specific plans for each one of our lives. In Jeremiah 29:11, we are told, "'For I know the plans I have for you,' declares the Lord, 'plans to prosper you and not to harm you, plans to give you hope and a future.'"[122] And Ephesians 3:20 reminds us, "Now to Him who is able to do immeasurably more than all we ask or imagine, according to His power that is at work within us."[123] As we take these two verses together, we learn that God has plans for our lives...beautiful plans...filled with hope...that will literally blow our imaginations.

So, if the Lord has these inconceivable plans for His children, then why must we wait for those plans to take shape? God makes us wait because He knows precisely when we are spiritually mature enough to receive bountiful blessings for our gain and His glory. "He is a wise gardener who 'waits for the land to yield its valuable crop' and 'is patient...for the autumn and spring rains.'"[124] God knows He cannot gather the harvest until it is ripe. "[W]aiting under the clouds of trials...will ultimately produce showers of blessings. Rest assured, that if God waits longer than we desire, it is simply to make the blessings doubly precious."[125]

Our Heavenly Father wants to bless us abundantly, but His plan and the blessings of obedience may take far more time than we expected. That's when we must remind ourselves that He is just like a loving parent who knows that we need to eat the substantive part of our meal before we get dessert. (Although the best part about being an adult is being able to have dessert first!) And He knows the perfect order and timing of both.

He also knows that waiting on Him will bring us far greater satisfaction when we get the answer for which we have been so faithfully waiting and praying. Waiting heightens the desire. Waiting focuses our heart. Waiting burrows that need down deep into our souls until it has become a part of us. And waiting on God deepens our faith and shows Him that we want Him far more than we want answers.

The cross is our direct proof that God doesn't always change the circumstances. He did not change them for His Only Son on that hillside where He was crucified. But the cross is also our proof that God always has a purpose behind the circumstances and that His purpose and His plan will prevail and triumph through every single circumstance every single time.

It may not be for me to see
The meaning and mystery
Of all that God has planned for me
Till "afterward"![126]

Chapter 4

What Waiting Requires of Us

Waiting on God is no task for the faint of heart. It requires a great deal from us, and often more than we believe we have in us to survive the day to day. Waiting on God requires us to have faith, patience, humility, courage, and perseverance. It requires each of these in abundant supply. So, let's look at each of these characteristics and why they are so crucial to us as we wait.

Faith

Waiting on God requires faith. What is faith? Faith can be defined as a "firm belief in something for which there is no proof"; "complete trust."[127] As we are told in Hebrews 11:1, faith can be defined as "confidence in what we hope for and assurance about what we do not see."[128]

C. S. Lewis defined faith as "the art of holding on to things your reasons once accepted, in spite of your changing moods." When our moods are flattened by everything we have believed will occur now seeming improbable and illogical, it is hanging-on faith that holds us on course and reminds us of the unfailing promises of God. For me, faith is that little light inside that continues to burn with hope urging me on, even though my own feelings are telling me to stop.

Levels of Faith

It has been said that there are three levels of faith in the Christian walk. The first level of faith believes when our emotions are positive, and we see signs to bolster those emotions. "Like Gideon, we feel the fleece and are willing to trust God if it is wet. This may be genuine faith, but it is imperfect. It is continually looking to feelings or some other sign instead of the Word of God. We have taken a great step toward maturity when we trust God without relying on our feelings. It is more of a blessing when we believe without experiencing any emotion."[129]

The second level of faith believes when all feelings are absent. This level of faith believes God even when the feelings have all dried up or when they have turned neutral towards the situation at hand. You just want the situation to come to an end in a way that God's will is done, and He gains the glory.

> And the third level transcends the other two, for it is faith that believes God and His Word when circumstances, emotions, appearances, people, and human reason all seem to urge something to the contrary. Paul exercised this level of faith when he said, "When neither sun nor stars appeared for many days and the storm continued raging, we finally gave up all hope of being saved" (Acts 27:20), then nevertheless went on to say, "Keep up your courage, men, for I have faith in God that it will happen just as He told me" (Acts 27:25). May God grant us faith to completely trust His Word, even when every other sign points the other way.[130]

Doubt and Faith

It is easy to trust God when life is going well and when we are on an emotional high, but how do we react when our world seems to be falling apart? How do we react when everything seems to be going against us and the promise that we believe God put in our hearts? Do our hearts fail us? Does our faith falter? Does doubt, like an uninvited guest, show up when our hope is failing? Does doubt lead us to question if God has forgotten about us? That our situation wasn't really that important to Him anyway? That we should move on from what He has promised and settle for "pretty good" instead of His best?

Even doubt can have its place in our waiting because as God reminds us in His Word, He uses *all* things for good...even doubt.

So, it's okay to have a bit of doubt in the middle of our stronghold of faith. It's okay to express our doubt to the Lord and ask for strength to double down in faith and hope. Because the reality is that if we aren't willing to entertain doubt's points, then our faith may never grow stronger as we tackle and then overcome those doubts that so desperately try to bring us down. As Paul Tournier has said, "Where there is no longer any opportunity for doubt, there is no longer any opportunity for faith."

Abraham was a great example to us of holding doubt at bay. Abraham hung on with hope and faith to all God had promised him and refused to let doubt whittle away at what he knew to be true. "Against all hope, Abraham in hope believed and so became the father of many nations, just as it had been said to him, 'So shall your offspring be.'"[131]

> Abraham's faith seemed to be in complete agreement with the power and constant faithfulness of Jehovah. By looking at the outer circumstances in which he was placed, he had no reason to expect the fulfillment of God's promise. Yet he believed the Word of the Lord and looked forward to the time when his descendants would be 'as numerous as the stars in the sky.[132]

Abraham's body was truly as good as dead since he was approximately a hundred years old. Sarah's womb had long gone barren. "Yet he did not waver through unbelief regarding the promise of God, but was strengthened in his faith and gave glory to God, being fully persuaded that God had power to do what He had promised."[133]

The Justification for Faith

Abraham held on in faith long after logic would have had him hang up his prayer mat. He continued in faith, and so should we. Why? I think there are three key reasons that we, like Abraham, should continue in faith until God's promises are delivered:

1.God does what He promises He will do.
2.Everything is possible for one who believes.
3.God is bigger than our situations.

Let's unwrap each one of these points.

God Does What He promises He Will Do

The first reason that we should hold on in faith until God's promises are delivered is that God does what He promises He will do. Period. There is no instance in biblical history where God made a promise and He failed to deliver. Repeatedly, God made a promise or multiple promises to His people and then delivered, above and beyond what they could have imagined.

These biblical faith highlights provide the foundation behind what we also see if we are willing to closely examine God's work in our own lives. Over and over, we see situation after situation that God has worked in, through, and around to produce what can only be described as miracles. Unfortunately, we are quick to forget what God has done for us in the past when we are staring in fear at the situation before us.

To fend off my own forgetfulness, I journal. I journal to record those instances when God came through...in the first hour or the eleventh hour...to lead me to victory. I know that recording those instances when God delivered me and answered my prayers when I had all but given up remind me that He is there, He is listening, and He cares. It may be something you find works for you as well.

And being able to look back on these journal entries may someday be the very difference between victory and defeat in our lives as we remind ourselves of God's faithfulness and grow in our confidence to hang on. We simply can't forget that God is faithful. God's faithfulness to us should spur on our faithfulness to Him and be our ever-present guard against discouragement.

To drive home the point, I found this incredible quote by Chuck Swindoll: "God never forgets anything He promises." That's right...

never. His agenda continues to unfold right on time, even when there is not the tiniest bit of evidence that He has heard us or that He remembers our cries.

Sometimes His timing seems delayed, and sometimes it truly does seem like He has forgotten us, but He hasn't. How could He possibly forget us? He knit us together in our very mothers' wombs. Psalm 139:13 says, "For you created my inmost being; you knit me together in my mother's womb."[134] He has counted every hair on our heads. He catches every tear we cry in a bottle.

Forgotten us? No! He is there. Waiting, watching, guiding, and orchestrating His plan for our lives as it unfolds one day at a time, one precious piece at a time.

Of course, we want to know the entire picture right now, and we are most especially interested in the ending. Now is the perfect time to come clean and admit that often we would love to fast forward to the end of the movie to find out what happens. We would love to read that last chapter and know how the story ends. And yes, we would love to skip dinner and just eat dessert first. (Or maybe that's just me!) Guilty as charged!

But God knows that the journey is as important as the ending. He knows we have a bit more growing to do before we see the ending. Perhaps He knows that if He revealed the ending before we were ready or even some of the steps in between, we might literally pass out. God knows when we will be ready, and He will lay out His plan for the piece parts of our lives when we are ready for it. And as we wait, our time at the foot of His throne, even that time spent in tears and suffering, will create an intimacy with Him that all the world's treasure could not buy.

Everything is Possible for One Who Believes

The second reason that we should hold on in faith until God's promises are delivered is as Mark 9:23 tells us, "[E]verything is possible for one who believes."[135] Believing takes asking, asking takes praying, and praying takes believing. Yes, one gigantic circle of believing prayer.

Mark 11:24 tells us exactly what believing prayer looks like. "Therefore I tell you, whatever you ask for in prayer, believe that you have received it, and it will be yours."[136] Believing prayer is prayer where we the confidence that what we have asked for, in accordance with God's will, we have received in that very moment. It may take some time to come to fruition, but God directs us to pray believing that our prayer has been answered.

Faith that believes it will see our prayers answered will keep us from becoming discouraged. "We will laugh at seemingly impossible situations while we watch with delight to see how God is going to open a path through our Red Sea. It is in these places of severe testing, with no human way out of our difficulty, that our faith grows and is strengthened."[137]

But sometimes, "everything" Mark 9:23 mentions we are praying for takes much longer to come than we might have expected. Sometimes, our believing prayer is just the first step, and the second and, unfortunately, much longer step is God training us in faith. And there are so many stages of learning in faith, including the "trial of faith, the discipline of faith, the patience of faith, and the courage of faith."[138]

Often God will require us to pass through many, if not all, of these stages before we realize the final result of faith—namely, the victory of faith.

There are times that God purposefully delays giving us His answer, and that delay is not a mistake. It is as much a part of the answer as the answer itself. Look at how God treated the spiritual greats of the Bible— Abraham, Moses, David, and Joseph—they were given promises, and then they waited. And their waiting faithfully took them through the incredible stages of faith, with the discipline of that faith equipping them for the work God had in store for them to accomplish.

Now don't get me wrong! "No amount of persecution will try you as much as experiences like these—ones in which you are required to wait on God. Once He has spoken His promise to work, it is truly hard to wait as you see the days go by with no fulfillment. Yet it is this discipline of faith that will bring you into a knowledge of God that would otherwise be impossible."[139] That knowledge of God will, in turn, strengthen our faith.

The reality of our faith is that it has nothing to do with our feelings, impressions, the appearance of things around us, or the possibility of the situation we are praying for coming to fruition.

> Faith rests on the pure Word of God alone. And when we take Him at His Word, our hearts are at peace. The closer we come to this point in our inner being, the more willing we are to leave ourselves in His hands and the more satisfied we are with all His dealings with us. Then when trials come, we will say, "I will patiently wait to see the good God will do in my life, with the calm assurance He will do it."[140]

God is Bigger Than Our Situation

The third reason that we should hold on in faith until God's promises are delivered is that God is bigger than our situation. In fact, the more impossible our situation appears to be, the bigger God will show Himself to be. You see, God is in the miracle-working business. What do you need? Seas parted? Water turned into wine? The sick healed? The dead raised? Yes, He has those and many others on His resume of miracles.

We simply need to come to Him and bring our bold faith that He can and does still work miracles. And we need to remind ourselves that God's thoughts are not our thoughts, and His ways are not our ways. Although our circumstances may look impossible, and our spirits to the point of being completely broken, we are called to "[r]emember the wonders He has done, His miracles."[141]

We should also remind ourselves that in almost every story of deliverance, it was individuals or groups of people coming to the point of desperation that presented a perfect opportunity for God to act. People arriving at "their wits' end"[142] of desperation was the beginning of God's power. That desperation often brings us to the end of ourselves, so the only place we have left to turn is to God.

God "generally waits to send His help until the time of our greatest need, so that His hand will be plainly seen in our deliverance. He chooses this method so we will not trust anything that we may see or feel, as we are so prone to do, but will place our trust solely on His Word—which we may always depend upon, no matter our circumstances.

Remember, the very time for faith to work is when our sight begins to fail. And the greater the difficulties, the easier it is for faith to work, for as long as we can see certain natural solutions to our problems, we will not have faith. Faith never works as easily when our natural prospects fail."[143]

God is the God of limitless resources, no matter what our situation looks like. The only limit He encounters is us. Our requests, our thoughts, our prayers are often too small, our dreams too limited, and our expectations pitifully low. God wants to raise our vision so we get a better understanding of who He is and what He can really do. And when we do, it will be impossible for us to measure the blessing He will bestow on us as He is "able to do immeasurably more than all we ask or imagine, according to His power that is at work within us."[144]

What Faith Will Require

Here is another one of those points you would probably rather not hear. Faith at times will require suffering and surrender. Surrendering everything to God is the highest form of faith, especially when it includes suffering. Dr. Charles Parkhurst said the following:

CHAPTER 4: WHAT WAITING REQUIRES OF US

The prophets and apostles could do amazing miracles, but they did not always do the will of God and thereby suffered as a result. Doing God's will and thus experiencing suffering is still the highest form of faith and the most glorious Christian achievement. Having your brightest aspirations as a younger person forever crushed; bearing burdens daily that are always difficult, and never seeing relief; finding yourself worn down by poverty while simply desiring to do good for others and provide a comfortable living for those you love; being shackled by an incurable physical disability; being completely alone, separated from those you love, to face the trauma of life alone; yet in all these, still being able to say through such a difficult school of discipline, "Shall I not drink from the cup of suffering my Father has given me?"—this is faith at its highest, and spiritual success at the crowning point. Great faith is exhibited not so much in doing as in suffering.[145]

What Faith Can Do

Although faith requires more than we think we can possibly give, it can also provide more than we ever imagined. Faith will help us rise from the ashes and start afresh. Faith will help us find the strength buried deep down inside our souls to make it one more day, despite our pain. Faith will help us focus on the sun that will soon be shining rather than the clouds that are currently blocking our vision. Faith will remind us that life is so much more than what our eyes are seeing. Faith will help us rise again.

Faith and Drop-Dead Dates

Faith can do so much in our lives, but faith cannot be given drop-dead dates. At one point during my time of waiting, someone asked what my drop-dead date was in terms of waiting for what I knew God had promised and when I would just move on. That question definitely resulted in me giving that person a head tilt as if to say, "What? Are you serious?" But I calmly asked, "Did Joseph give God a drop-dead date as to when he was going to lead Egypt? Did Moses give God a drop-dead date as to when he was going to stop wandering the wilderness? Did Abraham give God a drop-dead date on when his son was going to be born? No. Then I have equally as little right to give God a drop-dead date on when I will no longer be obedient."

We must walk in obedience until God is ready to bring His promises to fruition. Period. Of course, we get angry, sad, disappointed, and weary. But we still have to keep our faith: faith in God who is bigger than the most difficult of situations; faith in God who has given us specific promises; faith in God who has asked us to wait. So, we will continue to persevere with heroic endurance, even as our encouragers fall off the race path and ask us about our drop-dead dates, because we know joy will come in the morning, and it will be on God's timetable, not ours.

The Victory of Faith

Unfortunately, we can't learn faith in comfortable surroundings. Faith is one of those virtues that is only born in the school of hard knocks. "And it is in the atmosphere of conflict that faith finds its' most fertile soil and grows most rapidly to maturity."[146]

It is born where God's promises to us are met with Satan's tests and trials that appear to contradict all that God has spoken. And it is here, in the trials, where faith can stand firmly and declare loudly, "I have faith in God that it will happen just as he told me."[147]

> When nothing on which to lean remains,
> When strongholds crumble to dust;
> When nothing is sure but that God still reigns,
> That is just the time to trust
> It's better to walk by faith than sight,

In this path of yours and mine;
And the darkest night, when there's no outer light
Is the time for faith to shine.[148]

"Unbelief looks at God through the circumstances, just as we often see the sun dimmed by clouds or smoke. But faith puts God between itself and its circumstances and looks at them through Him."[149]

Trusting when it appears you have been forsaken; praying when it seems your words are simply entering a vast expanse where no one hears and no voice answers; believing that God's love is complete and that He is aware of your circumstances, even when your world seems to grind on as if setting its own direction and not caring for life or moving one inch in response to your petitions; desiring only what God's hands have planned for you; waiting patiently while seemingly starving to death, with your only fear being that you faith might fail—"this is the victory that has overcome the world"; this is genuine faith indeed.[150]

Patience

Waiting on God requires great patience, day in and day out. The definition of patience or being patient is "bearing pains or trials calmly or without complaint."[151] It has also been defined as "steadfast despite opposition, difficulty, or adversity."[152]

Philo called patience the "queen of virtues," perhaps because it can be the most difficult of character traits to practice (*Amen!*) and because it is so foundational for many other character traits. It is not an easy word to define as Barclay makes clear that "there is no single English word that transmits all the fullness of its meaning. The Greek word literally means, 'an abiding under,' and contains the ideas of steadfastness, constancy, staying power."[153]

Although some would like to define being patient as akin to simply waiting or passively resigning, biblical patience is an outgoing power of faith. Biblical patience is active energy and contains the quality of expectation. It is not just waiting, hoping God will answer. It is waiting, knowing He will.

Why is Patience So Important?

Why is patience so important? Patience is of crucial importance in our lives because it is the lynch pin behind our character development as Christians. We need patience for every single trial we face, every valley we go through, and every hard situation in which we find ourselves. Patience keeps us in the moment, and staying in the moment ensures that all those other crucial character traits have time to develop.

Now I would love to say that patience is the key to getting amazing blessings. Now, it is possible that our patience may very well result in some amazing blessings. But isn't the important thing not that we get the blessing or blessings, but that our Christ-like character is perfected? James tells us to count it all joy when we face various trials in James 1:2, but to do this, our character must mean more to us than our momentary comfort.

In our time of waiting, patience is key as we face difficult and, at times, soul-grinding trials. There are times in our lives when we have prayed and prayed, waited, and waited with still no evidence of God's answer raining down. As godly as we would like to be, we are also human, and there are times we simply want to give up. This is where patience comes in. Patience reminds us that God's timing is not our timing and what we think of as wasted time He sees as preparation time. Patience reminds us that there is no need to feel sad and discouraged. Our Creator knows our needs better than we do, and He has us in a season of waiting for a reason.

Patience also eliminates our self-works...and oh, I am so guilty of that! Why wait when I can just work harder, faster, or more efficiently?

But patience is about letting God work and handing back over to Him the little control I thought I might have had. (Did you hear the giggle?)

Finally, patience helps me hold steady in the midst of the storms I face. We need patience to hold us steady, so the lessons of those storms sink deep into our hearts. We need to let patience have the time to work on us!

There is no doubt that we can run ahead of God. We can try to control the situation that we are in. We may even be able to rush the unfolding of certain aspects of His will. But in doing so, we harm His work in the long run.

We have a perfect picture of this in the care of a rosebud. Rosebuds are exquisite in their color, shape, and design. If we are anxious to see what lies inside, we can force the opening of the rosebud. But as we do, we not only spoil the rosebud in its current form, we also spoil its future beauty as a fully blooming rose. So, as we are waiting, let's not force open the rosebud. Let's patiently wait on God's timing. Let's let His plan for our lives unfold in His perfect timing so that our blooming rose is a sight to behold!

Why is Patience So Hard?

Although I know how much I need patience in my life, and the Lord continues to remind me of that in countless situations, patience is not my strongest character trait. In fact, my motto for patience would fall more into the realm of "I would love to have more patience right now." Maybe not very model-Christian-like, but at least I am honest!

I can imagine I am not alone in my perpetual struggle with patience, and so I have to ask this question on all our behalf...why is patience so hard? Patience seems to be hard because it is so contrary to fallen humanity and how we naturally tend to think. The fact of the matter is that we want things right now. Not tomorrow, not a week from now, and definitely not a year from now. But patience requires putting aside our selfish desires and waiting in the moment.

Patience requires that we stop trying to shove something into this moment to find satisfaction. It requires recognizing that nothing, apart from the Lord, will provide us security, satisfaction, and significance. Nothing. Not that big job promotion, not that charming significant other, and not that prayed for a baby. (In fact, at some point, those things may very well eat away at our satisfaction and significance.) Nothing will fill our hearts and our void places like Jesus does.

Is it easy? For some people, perhaps, but for me, a resounding "no" on that survey question. For me, it takes constant renewal in the Word, prayer, and fellowship with the Lord, my sincere desire to change, and yes, even giving my loved ones permission to call me out gently and tactfully when I am being anything but patient. (I just wish it weren't so often!)

It's at this point that we must look ourselves in the mirror and ask, "Can I wait in patience, trusting God's wisdom for my life? Can I wait in patience without complaining and without questioning God's plan? Can I wait in patience, trusting that God is working in me, for my good, and for His glory?" Don't you just hate those tough questions! But if we are willing to answer yes, oh the amazing things God can do!

What Does Patience Look Like in the Real World?

As I have spent far more time than I cared to be patiently waiting, I found myself asking a key question. I understood the meaning of the Bible verses on patience, but the question still rattled in my head, "What does patience look like in the real world?"

I believe too often we misconstrue God's meaning of patience and waiting on Him as being stuck at a standstill. Waiting patiently, holding our ground against the enemy, and remaining obedient to God is hardly passive. It is active. Patience is a conscious act of the will.

I would even take this a step further. As we look at Hebrews 12:1, we are exhorted, "Let us run with patience the race that is set before us."[154] God brought this devotional to my attention one day, and I believe it described this act of "running with patience" so perfectly that I wanted to include it in its entirety.

Running "with patience" is a very difficult thing to do. The word "running" itself suggests the absence of patience or an eagerness to reach the goal. Yet we often associate patience with lying down or standing still. There is another kind of patience that I believe is harder to obtain—the patience that runs. Lying down during a time of grief or being quiet after a financial setback certainly implies great strength, but I know of something that suggests even greater strength—the power to continue working after a setback, the power to still run with a heavy heart, and the power to perform your daily tasks with deep sorrow in your spirit. This is a Christ-like thing.

Many of us could tearlessly deal with our grief if only we could do so in private. Yet what is so difficult is that most of us are called to exercise our patience not in bed but in the open street, for all to see. We are called upon to bury our sorrows not in restful inactivity but in active service—in our workplace, while shopping, and during social events—contributing to other people's joy. No other way of burying our sorrow is as difficult as this, for it is truly what is meant by running "with patience."

Dear Son of Man, this was Your kind of patience. It was both waiting and running at one time—waiting for the ultimate goal while in the meantime doing lesser work. I see You at Cana of Galilee, turning water into wine so the marriage feast would not be ruined. I see You in the desert, feeding the multitude with bread, simply to relieve a temporary need.

Yet all the time, You were bearing a mighty grief—not shared or spoken. Others may ask for a "rainbow in the clouds" (Genesis 9:13, NIV), but I would ask for even more from You. Make me, in my cloud, a rainbow bringing the ministry of joy to others. My patience will only be perfect when it works in Your vineyard.[155]

Being Patient Also Means Being Still

Although there are times God asks us to run with patience, there are also times that we are directed to be completely still and wait patiently. Psalm 37:7-9 says, "Be still before the LORD and wait patiently for Him."[156]

So, why do we need to be still? What is so important about stillness? The Bible appears to give us three reasons why we need to be still, and they are relatively simplistic: 1. So we can truly know God; 2. So we can allow God to work; and 3. So we can hear God speaking to our hearts.

The first reason we need to be still is so that we can truly know God. God Himself tells us in Psalm 46:10, "Be still, and know that I am God."[157] Being still, even in the midst of the storms raging in our lives, allows us time to get to know who God really is. It gives us time to reflect on history and all He did to intervene for His people in the most difficult of situations. It gives us time to study Scripture and to know, through His own words, just how much He loves us. It gives us time to let the depth of His love, that sent Him to the most painful death known to man, sink in and wash over us.

He is the great lover of our souls, and His love for us should provide the calm for our future. He is the ruler of heaven and earth and can put things into motion with a simple whisper or with no word at all. Despite His greatness, we struggle with being still.

Our lack of stillness and constant anxiety over where we are and where we are going can be likened to a family road trip. How many of us have been in a car on a long trip only to hear, "Are we there yet? Are we there yet?" about a hundred times? Okay, so maybe not a hundred times, but enough to drive us all a little nuts! And the answer I frequently heard was, "You need to sit back and enjoy the ride. We will be there soon enough."

Our lack of stillness and worry is exactly like asking God, "Are we there yet? Are we there yet?" And His answer to us, "Be still, and know that I am God." Translated into today's verbiage, "Sit back and enjoy the ride with Me. I want to spend time with just you. We will be there soon enough."

> The second reason we need to be still is that a quiet spirit allows God to work. A quiet spirit is of priceless value when performing outward activities. Nothing so greatly hinders the work of God's unseen spiritual forces, upon which our success in everything truly depends, as the spirit of unrest and anxiety.[158] There is tremendous power in stillness. A great believer once said, "All things come to him who knows how to trust and be silent." This fact is rich with meaning, and a true understanding of it would greatly change our ways of working. Instead of continuing our restless striving, we would "sit down" inwardly before the Lord, allowing the divine forces of His Spirit to silently work out the means to accomplish our goals and aspirations.[159]

"Restless striving"...ouch! I would even say "endless striving." Guilty as charged once again! I am a doer, and the very thought of "being still" goes against my very make-up and the essence of who I am. Even when I am sitting on the couch "resting," I am typically watching TV, reading a book, taking notes on the latest thing I have read, making a blanket, or perhaps doing all of the above simultaneously. I am good at *doing. I am not good* at being still, but I am working on it because I have realized that my endless striving and endless doing is just me striving to be in control. My doing provides me a security in and of itself, but it is a security that quickly fades as soon as a lull occurs, and I can't cross something else off my *to-do* list.

How neat is this though...God is the great "Doer"! God has asked us to wait, be patient, and be still because He wants to take control of the *doing*. He wants to make things happen for us that our own endless striving will never bring to fruition no matter how hard we try. For you other *doers* out there, being still and letting Him *do* may be the hardest thing you have ever had to do. And yes, you can even add that to your *to-do* list if it makes you feel better. But our not doing allows the great *Doer...to do* amazing things! So, let's put aside the *to-do* lists even for an hour or two, rest in the Lord, and realize that this time of rest is not wasted time. In fact, sometimes the times where we are the most productive are the times we are resting in Him in stillness.

Resting in God is exactly what this beautiful poem captures:
I laid it down in silence,
This work of mine,
And took what had been sent me –
A resting time.
The Master's voice had called me
To rest apart;
"Apart with Jesus only,"
Echoed my heart.
I took the rest and stillness
From His own hand,
And felt this present illness
Was what He planned.
How often we chose labor,
When He says "Rest" –
Our ways are blind and crooked;
His way is best.

Work He Himself has given,
He will complete.
There may be other errands
For tired feet;
There may be other duties
For tired hands,
The present is obedience
To His commands.
There is a blessed resting
In lying still,
In letting His hand mold us,
Just as He will.
His work must be completed,
His lesson set;
He is the Master Workman:
Do not forget!
It is not only "working"
We must be trained;
And Jesus "learned" obedience,
Through suffering gained.
For us, His yolk is easy,
His burden is light.
His discipline most needful,
And all is right.
We are to be His servants;
We never choose
If this tool or if that one
Our hands will use
In working or in waiting
May we fulfill
Not our at all, but only
The Master's will![160]

God not only wants to just *do* for us, He wants to *fight* for us. In fact, Exodus 14:14 says, "The Lord will fight for you; you need only to be still."[161] I don't know about you, but it gets me a little choked up when one of my family or friends fights for me. It gives me a renewed energy when they go to bat for me, defend me, and have my back. And as much as I love them to pieces, their ability to fight for me pales in comparison to the fight the God of the Universe can bring to the ring. Plus, He has an endless source of energy, so He will never stop fighting.

Even when we know God wants us to be still, that He wants to be the One to do something for us, and that He wants to fight for us, there are so many times we struggle with being still in body and mind. Getting our bodies to be still is at times challenging, but sheer exhaustion as we have run ourselves into the ground once again can help us get still rather quickly. Sound familiar?

How often do we find it's not our bodies that present the obstacle to being still, but rather our minds? There are times I may be physically drained of every bit of energy I have, and yet my mind will be running like it's an Olympic sprinter. (Sadly, I have yet to win an Olympic Gold Medal.) What I have realized is that when my mind is racing like that, I am still striving to make myself feel secure. I am relying on my own thinking and my own ability to "solve" my way out of whatever predicament I find myself in, rather than handing it over to the Lord in surrender.

So, what do we do? What do we do when, during our times of waiting, the "spiritual storm" rages within us? What do we do when our mind continues to run the hundred-meter race, even when we have taken off our track shoes?

How do we quiet our frantic, anxious minds? *We stop*—stop scheming, stop searching for answers, stop manipulating, and stop doing. *We start* praying for the intervention of the Holy Spirit to control our minds and soothe us from the inside out. We recognize the *power of stillness* as Jesus did, even in the face of false accusers, and we let God fight for us. And we recognize the greatest promise of all, that no matter what storms rage within and around us, we know that God cannot and will not break His word to us. Because the reality is that God wants to teach us how to weather that storm so that even when the situation itself hasn't changed, we can still find peace.

The third reason we need to be still is so that we can hear God speaking to our hearts. Too often, God brings a time of waiting, and we try to fill that waiting time with busyness. The enemy fills our heads with lies about how we must act, stop doing nothing, take matters into our own hands, and move out in the direction that we think is best. But being still is not doing "nothing," and it is a thousand times harder than rushing headlong into life's busyness that is constantly beckoning to us. Being still is slowing down, getting some separation from our day-to-day circumstances and activities, concentrating on God, and recognizing that is then He will be able to speak into our hearts.

Too often, the clutter and ambient noise of our own lives deafen us to His still quiet voice trying to speak into our lives. When we get alone with Him, the noise and the lights of our worlds are dimmed, and the opinions of others stop ringing in our heads. When we get alone with Him and have the courage to wait in silent expectation, He will open our hearts and our minds in ways we had not imagined as He whispers to us.

I thought this very personal example from a writer perfectly captured how being still is the only way for us to truly hear God.

Inner stillness is an absolute necessity to truly knowing God. I remember learning this during a time of great crisis in my life. My entire being seemed to throb with anxiety, and the sense of need for immediate and powerful action was overwhelming. Yet the circumstances were such that I could do nothing, and the person who could have helped would not move.

For a time, it seemed as if I would fall to pieces due to my inner turmoil. Then suddenly, "a still small voice" (1 Kings 19:12) whispered in the depths of my soul, "Be still, and know that I am God" (Psalm 46:10). The words were spoken with power, and I obeyed. I composed myself, bringing my body to complete stillness, and forced my troubled spirit into quietness. Only then, while looking up and waiting, did I know that it was God who had spoken. He was in the midst of my crisis and my helplessness, and I rested on Him.

This was an experience I would not have missed for anything. I would also say it was from the stillness that the power seemed to arise to deal with the crisis, and that very quickly brought it to a successful resolution. It was during the crisis, I effectively learned that my "strength is to sit still."[162]

Our waiting and being still can even take us one step farther as waiting......upon God is vital to see Him and receive a vision from Him. And the amount of time spent before Him is also critical, for our hearts are like a photographer's film— the longer exposed, the deeper the impression. For God's vision to be impressed on our hearts, we must sit in stillness at His feet for quite a long time. Remember, the troubled surface of a lake will not reflect an image.

Yes, our lives must be quiet and peaceful if we expect to see God. And the vision we see from Him has the power to affect our lives in the same way a lovely sunset brings peace to a troubled heart. Seeing God always transforms human life.[163]

What is the Outcome of Being Patient and Being Still?

When we have come to the point of complete stillness in our time of waiting, we will find ourselves waiting for God's leading in everything we do. We will eagerly watch for the slightest movement on His part, keeping ourselves ever faithful to His leading, knowing that anything that is not in perfect alignment with His will is simply a waste of our time. We will strain our ears to hear the slightest whisper He utters. We will find that our waiting and our stillness reveals untapped resources for which God provides to us to cope with each day as we wait.

We will also find that our waiting in stillness has provided a fertile field in which the fruits of the Spirit have had a chance to grow. Those fruits do not grow with the same intensity when all is well in our lives. It is the storms and trials that pummel us that intensify the growth to maturity and leave us with a completely different harvest than when we started into our trial.

Nothing can touch our hearts like the power of stillness.

For the hearts that will cease focusing on themselves, there is "the peace of God, which transcends all understanding" (Philippians 4:7)[164]; "quietness and trust" (Isaiah 30:15)[165], which is the source of all strengths; a "'great peace' that will never "make them stumble" (Psalm 119:165)[166]; and a deep rest, which the world can never give nor take away. Deep within the center of the soul is a chamber of peace where God lives and where, if we will enter it and quiet all other sounds, we can hear His "gentle whisper."[167] There is only one way to know God: "Be still, and know."[168]

Humility

Waiting on God requires humility, and our humility is shown through our obedience to do what God has called us to do. Humility is defined as "a quality by which a person considering his own defects has a humble opinion of himself and willingly submits himself to God and to others for God's sake."[169] Obedience or to "obey" can be defined as "to follow the commands or guidance of"; "to conform or comply with."[170] Our humility in waiting demonstrates itself as we willingly submit to God and follow His guidance in each and every step He lays out for us.

We Are Called to Obedience

Whether we want to acknowledge it or not, we are called to obedience. Verse after verse in the Bible calls us to obedience to God. Deuteronomy 8:6 tells us to "Observe the commands of the Lord your God, walking in obedience to him and revering Him."[171] Deuteronomy 10:12 asks us, "[W]hat does the Lord your God ask of you but to fear the Lord your God, to walk in obedience to Him, to love Him, to serve the Lord your God with all your heart and with all your soul?"[172]

And those verses are followed by verses that remind us of how God will treat us when we are obedient. First Kings 11:38 promises us, "If you do whatever I command you and walk in obedience to Me and do what is right in my eyes by obeying my decrees and commands, as David My servant did, I will be with you."[173] Psalm 128:1 tells us, "Blessed are all who fear the Lord, who walk in obedience to Him."[174] Jeremiah 7:23 tells us, "Walk in obedience to all I command you, that it may go well with you."[175]

Each one of these verses calls us to obedience to God. We are not called to figure out who, what, when, and where of our circumstances. We are called to simply obey.

Sometimes, God must get us to the point of total brokenness before we give Him our total obedience. When we get to that point, despite the pain we feel day in and day out, we are willing to do whatever God has called us to do. The beauty of this situation is that when God calls us to do something, especially when we don't want to do it, there is always a reason.

Obedience is Hard, and It Hurts

So, I am going to say what you probably don't want to hear and what others don't want to tell you. Obedience is hard, and sometimes it hurts. I suppose for too long now I have held the Sunday school view of obedience in that once you obeyed, the blessings would just come showering down right then. What I have learned is that obedience will bring blessings, but it may very well bring difficulty and suffering first.

The story of Joseph reminds us that obedience can bring difficulty before it brings blessings. In one of his trials, Joseph did what was right by denying the advances of the wife of his employer. Instead of blessings, he received imprisonment for many years. He suffered greatly for being obedient to God's commands.

At this time in my life, I know that I am being obedient in a way that I have never been before, and I, too, have found myself in what can best be described as a prison of suffering. I have laid down my plans, my pride, and have obeyed even when what I am doing may appear to others to be foolish. I know that it has cost me more than I ever thought I would be willing to give, and the price is my very heart and soul. I know that one day this storm will end, and my joy will be restored, and like to Job, God too will give me a double portion. But for now, I suffer in an anguish I have never felt, with tears that never seem to end, with a heart no closer to healing than it was many months ago. This is the darkest of nights, and there is no light of day in sight. And still, I trust and obediently wait.

Despite the anguish, my obedience and yours during this waiting time can best be described as our surrendering of what we want for God's best for us. Surrendering is best demonstrated in total and complete obedience. When we are obedient, we follow God's Word, even if it doesn't make sense. Even when it's hard. Even when it hurts. We know we have fully surrendered to God when we take our hands "off the wheel" and trust Him to work things out instead of trying to manipulate others, force our agenda, and control the situation. Surrendering is letting go and letting God work. Instead of trying harder, we trust more. And that's when we God can and will use us, and victory then comes through our surrender. Seems paradoxical, but we have a paradoxical type of God. So, the best thing we can do is surrender our past regrets, our present problems, our future plans, our fears, dreams, weaknesses, habits, and hurts. (I think you get the point!) It's time we surrender our past, present, and future.

But surrendering isn't easy, and obediently waiting isn't always fun. Sometimes it feels like God is giving us a "Holy Time Out." It feels like a test of our endurance as the pain we feel is magnified each day, and our prayers go unanswered. It requires daily surrender to God's timetable and not our own. In fact, it seems that waiting on God is one of the hardest tests we Christians will ever face.

In those minutes, the days, the months, the years of waiting continue to tick by, we have to continue to be obedient and cling to our faith. God is working a far bigger plan than we can see with our short-term view, and He loves us more than we can possibly imagine.

God's Promise When We are Obedient

Regardless of the why, we need to continue in humility to be obedient and wait until God's promises are fulfilled. What we will find is that when we obey God's voice and surrender to Him whatever we hold dearest to our hearts, He will multiply it over and over and over again.

Abraham understood this concept firsthand when the Lord directed Him to offer up his son Isaac as a sacrifice. For Abraham to give up his one and only son meant he would not lay down every desire and dream he had for Isaac's life, but it also meant that the legacy God promised Him would disappear with no heir. Graciously, God provided a sacrificial lamb in lieu of Isaac's life, restored Isaac to his father, and Abraham's family became "as numerous as the stars in the sky and as the sand on the seashore." And through his descendants, "when the set time had fully come, God sent His Son" (Galatians 4:4).[176]

This is exactly how God deals with every child of His when we truly sacrifice. We surrender everything we own and accept poverty—then He sends wealth. We leave a growing area of ministry at His command—then He provides one better than we had ever dreamed. We surrender all our cherished hopes and die to self—then He sends overflowing joy and His "life, and have it abundantly" (John 10:10).[177][178]

Abraham's experience was not unique or isolated.

It is only an example and a pattern of how God deals with those who are prepared to obey Him whatever the cost. "And so, having patiently waited, he obtained the promise" (Hebrews 6:15),[179] and so will you. The moment of your greatest sacrifice will also be the precise moment of your greatest and most miraculous blessing. God's river, which never runs dry, will overflow its banks, bringing you a flood of wealth and grace. Indeed, there is nothing God will not do for those who will dare to step out in faith onto what appears to be only a mist. As they take their first step, they will find a rock beneath their feet.[180]

Your sacrifice of praise and your sacrificial obedience have not gone unnoticed by God. There is *no* sacrifice you could make to Him that will not be met with a totally disproportionate response of His great love, and grace and provision! Any gift you give, any offering you make, and initiative you take to obey Him when it costs you will be responded to in ways you cannot imagine. He is a disproportionate God! Understand your wealth in Him. Though you feel the pain of this sacrifice now, get a vision for the response He is preparing for you!

Some of you are making huge sacrifices for His Name's sake. Some of you could so easily grab for yourself a counterfeit version of something He has promised you, but ultimately, you really want to wait for God's best for you. Wait for God's best and see if He won't absolutely blow your mind with His goodness, His grace, and His attention to detail.

If at all possible, get your eyes off what it's costing you right now, and lift your eyes to the Heavens, your unlimited supply. If you're lacking in strength or perspective, get alone with God. Spend extended time camping in His presence. Open your hands to receive more of what He so lovingly wants to give. Remind yourself of His Word and His promise to you. Strengthen yourself in Him by reminding yourself who you are to *him!*

There is no gift you can give, no prayer you can pray, no act of obedience that you can initiate that will not be met by overwhelming love, provision, goodness, grace, and power. You may not see its evidence right away, but it's there, affecting change, making a difference, and moving mountains. One day your eyes will see it. So know it now. Stand on the faithfulness of your God *now*. Today. Believe Him for big things. Entrust your cares, your sacrifices, and your gifts to Him.[181]

Obedience Punctuated

I had the obedience issue punctuated for me in a very dramatic way regarding my job. I had loyally worked for a company for about ten years and saw sweeping changes (not all good) occurring. Unfortunately, I found myself in a position where I was being asked to do things that went against my values as a leader and was being asked to lead in a way I felt was disrespectful to my people.

As hard as I tried to fight through it, I found the position I was being placed in taking a toll on my soul. At that point, I started praying that the Lord would just make it extremely evident to me whether I was to leave the company or stay. In fact, I remember specifically praying, "Lord, if You want me to leave this company, please just make it abundantly clear to me, and I will go wherever You would have me go." It was a decision I wrestled with as I wanted to do what was right for my team, I wanted to do what was right for my future, and I have always been extremely loyal to my employer.

The Lord absolutely answered my prayer, but not in the way I expected it. In fact, the day my prayer was answered is seared in my mind. I was eating lunch with my best friend from high school when my boss at the time called me. A call from him was rare, so I knew something dramatic was about to happen. It was at that point he offered me a lateral job in New York City, with the caveat that he no longer had room for me on his team.

It's a bit of a life-changing moment (to say the least) when you go from being on the fast track of a company to being told your boss has no room for you on his team. Now granted, I still had a job, but that job would be in New York City. As much as I enjoy visiting New York, it was not where I wanted to live or the city in which I one day hoped to make my home.

So, I listened as my boss talked about the new job and who my new boss would be, and I suddenly had this overwhelming peace. I knew this was my sign that it was time to go, and New York was not where God was sending me.

As my boss finally posed the question of whether or not I was interested in this new position, I calmly answered, "I thank you for the consideration, but I am not interested in going to New York." You could literally have heard a pin drop. More discussion ensued as that was not the answer he had expected to hear. But I just knew this was my prayer answered and God's way of telling me it was time to go.

I walked back into lunch with my friend and calmly said, "I just ended my career at my current company." She just about fell on the floor.

Approximately a month later, I left the company I had given ten solid, wonderful years of my life with no regrets.

Now, just in case this wasn't abundantly clear, I left with no job lined up. *No job!* I had worked since I was twelve years old in all sorts of different jobs but never left a job without having another one lined up. Scary? Of course! I had a mortgage and bills and no one else to depend on and helping to make ends meet but myself.

And yet, I felt a peace I never felt before. I had specifically asked God to show me if I was supposed to stay with my current company, He provided the direction, and I obediently followed. I just knew He would take care of me. It was the "how" it would all work out that I just couldn't wait to see.

To wrap up the story, I made finding a job my new full-time job. I religiously started networking, going to networking events, applying for jobs, and polishing up my resume. I knew I at least had to be active in the pursuit of a job, and God would guide me from there.

In my third month of job searching, I took an interview with a company in Michigan. On my return flight home on a fairly good size plane, my seatmate was a woman who turned out to be a VP of a Fortune-Fifty company. We hit it off, she asked for my resume, and by the next morning, she had emailed me to come in for an interview.

Was it a coincidence that I took that interview in Michigan? Was it a coincidence that she had been rerouted from Texas to Detroit and was my seatmate? Was it a coincidence that I tried to get on an earlier flight home and was unable to? No; in God's plans, there are no such things as coincidences!

The result of my obedience was that I had four months of amazing closeness with the Lord...I really had nowhere else to turn; I ended up in an entirely new industry working for a great company, and I had a boss that could not have been more thrilled to have me on the team. Was that four-month period one of the scariest of my life? Absolutely! Did doubts creep up on me, and did I find myself asking the question, "What have I done?" Absolutely! But my faith in God's promises to those who are obedient won out, and He proved His faithfulness once again.

Courage

Waiting on God requires courage and courage in a big way. So, what is courage? Courage can be defined as "mental or moral strength to venture, persevere, and withstand danger, fear, or difficulty."[182]

Although it may sound strange, our waiting on the Lord requires great courage in three different ways. First, we need it to resist the temptation to just give in, give up, or accept less than God's best. Second, it takes courage to disregard the negative words of those around us, as well-meaning as they may try to be. Third, it takes courage to stand firm against our own fear of failure.

First, we need courage to resist the temptation to give in, give up, and accept less than God's best. It takes courage to press on when easy alternatives are offered up or our emotions are just starting to get the best of us. It takes courage to stand and wait, without losing heart or hope, in submission to God's will.

Second, it takes courage to disregard the negative words of those around us. Even those we love and admire can try to sway us out of doing what we know God has called us to do. I know there were a few people encouraging me to take the job in New York City, but I just knew that wasn't where God wanted me.

And let's look at Noah. I can only imagine the negative statements hurled at him as he built an ark in the middle of nowhere with not a raindrop in sight. Thankfully, Noah had great courage, and he "did all the Lord commanded him" to do.[183]

Third, it takes courage to stand firm against our own fear of failure. It takes an amazing amount of courage to hold onto God's promises when absolutely nothing seems to be happening in the direction of our dreams. It takes courage to tamp down our own doubts and insecurities as we look toward the future and what is to come. It takes courage to go the way God wants us to go, even when we are uncertain of victory on the other end or what it will look like when we find it.

To me, courage is strength in the face of pain or grief. Talk about hitting me right in the heart! It has also been defined as "the quality of mind or spirit that enables a person to face difficulty, danger, pain, etc., without fear."[184]

Why is it so important to be without fear? Fear stops us in our tracks. I mean dead in our tracks! We have all heard the saying "like a deer in headlights," right? Well, the deer stopped because the deer was scared to death. The deer was afraid, just like we so often do.

God recognizes that we humans can be like a deer in headlights too when our hearts are struck with fear. So, in Joshua 1:9, He says, "Have I not commanded you? Be strong and courageous. Do not be afraid; do not be discouraged, for the LORD your God will be with you wherever you go."[185] Isaiah 41:10 repeats this command and promise by saying, "So do not fear, for I am with you; do not be dismayed, for I am your God. I will strengthen you and help you; I will uphold you with my righteous right hand."[186] Isaiah 41:13 confirms it once again by stating, "For I am the LORD your God who takes hold of your right hand and says to you, Do not fear; I will help you."[187] And the icing on the cake is Hebrews 13:5-6, "Never will I leave you; never will I forsake you. So, we say with confidence, 'The Lord is my helper; I will not be afraid. What can mere mortals do to me?'"[188]

But God promises far more than just being with us, strengthening us, or helping us. Isaiah 43:1b-2 firmly states, "Do not fear, for I have redeemed you; I have summoned you by name; you are mine. When you pass through the waters, I will be with you; and when you pass through the rivers, they will not sweep over you. When you walk through the fire, you will not be burned; the flames will not set you ablaze."[189] This verse claims protection for us as we walk through the most difficult of times—through the waters of waiting, through the rivers of pain, through the fire of trials and suffering—He is right there. We will not be overcome.

The beauty in all of this is that when we seek the Lord and lay our fears before Him, He helps vanquish those fears. Psalm 34:4 says, "I sought the Lord and He answered me; He delivered me from all my fears."[190] He wants to be our knight in shining armor delivering us from the dragon that embodies our fears. Exodus 14:13 touts that deliverance again by saying, "Do not be afraid. Stand firm and you will see the deliverance the Lord will bring you today."[191]

Until our deliverance comes, we must stand strong and courageous. We must fight against discouragement. We must at times act despite our emotions, which may be all over the map, and press on. We must not compromise our convictions. We must not let our fear displace our faith. And when we feel ourselves growing weak, we have a choice—to fall into the pit of despair or to fix our focus on Christ, who beckons us one more step. With each step we take, we are one day closer to our prayers getting answered and one day closer to a breakthrough.

When we find it difficult to take the next step, and when our fears are sapping every last ounce of courage that we have left, we need to go back to the Lord and ask for His strength to help us stand in the face of our grief and pain and fight one more day. At times we will wake up to another day, and we won't know if we can face the fears staring us down. And so, we simply must stand up to that day and stand on what we know to be true. We must stand firm on God's promises. We must keep fighting the fight of faith, and we must dig deep down to find the courage that will help us win the war on waiting. Stand firm Treasured One, for God will provide deliverance.

Perseverance

Waiting on God also requires intense perseverance. So, what is perseverance? Perseverance is "continued effort to do or achieve something despite difficulties, failure, or opposition."[192] It can also be defined as "steady persistence in a course of action, a purpose, a state, etc., especially in spite of difficulties, obstacles, or discouragement."[193] I would personally define perseverance as steady persistence in moving forward toward a goal, despite the pain.

In our time of waiting, we tend to feel like we have embarked on a mountain size uphill journey with no peak in sight. No light at the end of the tunnel. No finish line to speak of. We are faced with another day of moving forward, one step at a time. (Although sometimes I swear the mountain is an escalator, and I am running up the downside!)

Thankfully, along the way, God grants us places of ease and rest. Although we are still on the mountain and we are still climbing, we see places where God allows the pain of our waiting to be dulled for a few minutes, a few hours, or even a full day. I had a day like that recently with a friend of mine where we tandem kayaked down the Potomac River, biked through mud puddles along a railroad track like we were little kids, ate hot fudge ice cream Sundaes in a quaint little town, and saw two owls in the wild. It was glorious. And for that day, my pain was eased. Unfortunately, until we finally crest that mountain peak, the dulled pain will return, and it will require our perseverance to keep moving forward despite it.

Moving forward despite the pain requires endurance, but perseverance is far more than just enduring something. As Oswald Chambers says, "It is endurance combined with absolute assurance and certainty that what we are looking for is going to happen. Perseverance means more than just hanging on, which may be only exposing our fear of letting go and falling. Perseverance is our supreme effort of refusing to believe that our hero is going to be conquered.

Our greatest fear is not that we will be damned, but that somehow Jesus Christ will be defeated."[194]

Jesus Himself persevered through pain unfathomable to the human mind so that He would reach the goal of conquering death and providing us eternal life. And He calls us to persevere as well. But why? Why do we need to persevere in whatever trial God has laid before us?

First, we persevere because perseverance must finish its work in us. James 1:2-4 tells us, "Consider it pure joy, my brothers and sisters, whenever you face trials of many kinds, because you know that the testing of your faith produces perseverance. Let perseverance finish its work so that you may be mature and complete, not lacking anything."[195] When we persevere, James encourages us by telling us that its result will leave us "mature and complete, not lacking anything."

Exploring that idea more deeply, part of that maturity and completeness is the building of our character. Romans 5:3-4 says, "Not only so, but we also glory in our sufferings, because we know that suffering produces perseverance; perseverance, character; and character, hope."[196] There is no greater goal in life, other than glorifying God, to be a man or woman of great character. And perseverance is the vehicle that gets us there.

Secondly, we must continue to persevere so that we receive what God has promised. As Hebrews 10:35-36 says, "So do not throw away your confidence; it will be richly rewarded. You need to persevere so that when you have done the will of God, you will receive what He has promised."[197] If we give up, we literally may be quitting the race one step short of the finish line and miss a spectacular God-given blessing. We must keep going!

So, how do we keep going? How do we persevere? We simply choose to keep going. Persevering is a mental exercise unlike any other. Even when we are in the throes of pain and suffering, we can choose to keep going. Even when our emotions are taking us on a roller coaster ride that we were beyond ready to get off five rides ago, we can choose to continue pressing forward. As we press forward, we need to remind ourselves that what we are going through is God's way of perfecting us so that we lack *nothing!*

Now I know that the waiting—the gut-wrenching, heart-shredding, tear-inducing waiting—can be difficult to see past. Rather than jumping up and down with joy over the perfecting God is doing in my own life, I tend to find myself broken, humbled, weeping, and with my face on the ground begging God for mercy. That's when God's promises hit my heart, and I know that if I continue to persevere and fight the good fight, I will be blessed, and I will reap a harvest. James 1:12 reminds us we will be blessed if we persevere. It states, "Blessed is the one who perseveres under trial because, having stood the test, that person will receive the crown of life that the Lord has promised to those who love Him."[198] Galatians 6:9 speaks to the harvest we will reap in reminding us, "Let us not become weary in doing good, for at the proper time we will reap a harvest if we do not give up."[199]

I love how good God is in giving us Bible examples of those who persevered and refused to give up. Three in particular strike my heart in Job, the persistent widow, and Jesus. James 5:11 brings us to Job as it says, "As you know, we count as blessed those who have persevered. You have heard of Job's perseverance and have seen what the Lord finally brought about. The Lord is full of compassion and mercy."[200] Job persevered through unimaginable suffering, and God blessed him abundantly for his faithfulness.

Luke 18:1-6 provides us a beautiful parable about the persistent widow. It states,

> Then Jesus told his disciples a parable to show them that they should always pray and not give up. He said: "In a certain town there was a judge who neither feared God nor cared what people thought. And there was a widow in that town

who kept coming to him with the plea, 'Grant me justice against my adversary.' For some time, he refused. But finally he said to himself, 'Even though I don't fear God or care what people think, yet because this widow keeps bothering me, I will see that she gets justice, so that she won't eventually come and attack me!'" And the Lord said, "Listen to what the unjust judge says. And will not God bring about justice for His chosen ones, who cry out to Him day and night? Will He keep putting them off? I tell you, He will see that they get justice, and quickly. However, when the Son of Man comes, will He find faith on the earth?"[201]

The widow refused to give up until she was given justice. She persevered day in and day out until the judge realized there would be no relief from her visits and pleadings. She knew that the judge could not put her off forever. We must have the same persevering faith that God will hear our pleadings, and He will give us justice in our obedience.

Hebrews 12:1-4 focuses on Jesus and helps us clearly see the perseverance He exhibited throughout His life.

Therefore, since we are surrounded by such a great cloud of witnesses, let us throw off everything that hinders and the sin that so easily entangles. And let us run with perseverance the race marked out for us, fixing our eyes on Jesus, the pioneer and perfecter of faith. For the joy set before Him He endured the cross, enduring its shame, and sat down at the right hand of the throne of God. Consider Him who endured such opposition from sinners, so that you will not grow weary and lose heart.[202]

It is tough to keep going and keep persevering when we are weary and our hearts are heavy. When our strength is gone, the next step requires more energy than we can muster, and our brains have called out sick for the week—there is one thing that can motivate us to keep moving forward. Jesus. Perseverance is born out of our faith in Jesus and knowing that He will do all He has promised to do.

Our own determination, desires, dreams, and drive will run out and will not be enough to keep us moving on this uphill journey. But our faith in Him will. He healed the sick, gave sight to the blind, calmed raging seas, turned water into wine, multiplied five loaves and two fish to feed a crowd, and raised the dead. Our faith in Him and His ability to perform miracles will keep us showing up one more day, to take one more step until our journey is completed.

Thankfully, we know that one day our waiting will come to an end, and there is "light that is coming for the heart that holds on."[203] Sometimes that waiting will require us persevering with the help of those we love, and sometimes it will mean that we are persevering alone. Oftentimes other people may think we are crazy to persevere in what appears to be a time of endless waiting with no hope in sight. But we know that every heartfelt desire, every hope, every dream of our minds will be fulfilled if it is noble and aligned with God's will.

In the meantime, here are some great quotes from which we can gain a little source of encouragement—or a laugh—from:

"If you are going through hell, keep going" (Winston S. Churchill).

"When you get to the end of your rope, tie a knot and hang on" (FDR).

"Do not get discouraged—it may be the last key on the ring that opens the door."[204]

"When you are down to nothing, God is up to something."[205]

We simply must persevere. We must finish this race so that we are "mature and lacking nothing." We must persevere so that we can be the recipients of what God has promised. Even when we are beyond tired and beyond weary, we must let our faith in Jesus propel us forward.

Staying in the Neutral Zone

Waiting also requires us to stay in the "neutral zone." What I mean by that is that as we wait, our emotions can take such drastic positive and negative swings that it can almost be debilitating. So, to guard ourselves against the very difficult emotional highs and lows, we must do our best to stay in the neutral zone of emotions. In doing that, we must avoid hanging on too tightly to either the affirming or downright negative events we experience during this time of waiting. We must keep focused on the big picture.

If we allow ourselves to get too emotionally high, we will have far further to fall when Satan makes his next attack. If we allow ourselves to get too emotionally low, we may not be able to drag ourselves up out of the hopeless pit to cope with a normal day. But if we stay in the neutral zone until the season of waiting is over and God has fulfilled His promise, we can survive with most of our sanity in tack.

I recently walked through what I deem the toughest time I have ever faced in my life thus far. I had been called to obey God in an area of my life and had done so even though it was difficult, scary, and far more emotional than I could have ever imagined.

As I waited obediently, I spent a great deal of time sharing my heart with those who were nearest and dearest to me and who I knew were trustworthy. Some of that time was spent sharing with them the little things that seemed to be God's way of letting me know I was still on the right path. There were times I experienced elation as the smallest, seemingly insignificant event sparked eternal hope in me once again. Other times, I shared my anger, my hurt, my disappointment, and my longing for the pain to stop. At times the desire to give up, throw in the towel, and disobey was overwhelming. The doubts hit, trying to convince me that I was simply going to drown in this ocean of waiting with no lighthouse in sight.

Interestingly, these emotions could all hit in a single day. Talk about exhausting! The unpredictable swells of my emotions had me pleading for the dry land of emotional stability. My life jacket of obedience often seemed to be my only source of solace, although at times, it too even seemed a bit too snug. I was doing what God asked me to do, and He would fulfill His promise, but this was far from my idea of God's just rewards for obedience.

Doing what God asked me to do was hard, but it became easier when I stayed in the neutral zone and exercised emotional self-control. God was working things out on His timeline and in His way. When I trusted Him explicitly and exercised emotional self-control, the waves seemed to level out one by one, if even just temporarily.

It is so difficult to walk that emotional line between fear and the promise being fulfilled, but that's where faith comes in. Hebrews 11:1 reminds us, "Faith is the substance of things hoped for and the evidence of things unseen."[206] Faith in God can allow our dreams to become a reality.

I promise you, the storm will blow over. The waves will cease. Dry land will come into view. God will fulfill the promises He has made to us in ways that leave us speechless. Let go. Trust Him. Stay in the neutral zone with faith, patience, humility, courage, and perseverance.

Chapter 5

The Consequences of Not Waiting

Whenever God asks us to wait on Him, we have a couple of options. One option is to try to manipulate the circumstances we find ourselves in. It's our weak attempt to control a situation that most likely leaves us rather fearful. Most of us have done it before, either consciously or subconsciously. But by being manipulative, we may forfeit God's best for us and may even create a situation where more heartache will follow.

Another option is that we can disobey God and walk in our own path—most likely in the exact opposite direction He has asked us to go. If He has asked us to be still and wait, we may decide we have had enough and move forward pursuing our dreams in whatever manner we believe to be the best. Unfortunately, the Holy Spirit's tugging on our hearts never quite seems to stop until we turn around and do the right thing. The Holy Spirit is rather relentless on that front.

Another option is that we can walk away from God altogether. We may simply decide that He has had us waiting long enough, and therefore, He simply isn't the God we believed Him to be. Unfortunately, our walking away leaves a void that we will try to fill with anything and everything that even resembles a fit. But we can't fill the God-sized void left behind, and so we will struggle with a lack of peace deep in our souls that nothing will be able to satisfy.

Although the options are different, the consequences of choosing any of these three and not waiting on God are the same. If we choose any option other than waiting on God, we will find ourselves disappointed, put ourselves in harm's way, not experience God's very best, and hurt those we love. We may think God needs our help in manipulating the circumstances, so everything turns out just "right," and so we justify our disobedience. But our plans, due to their disobedient nature, will only lead to more disappointment and further frustration.

We will also put ourselves in harm's way by stepping outside of God's will. By following what we believe to be our own well-thought-out plans, we may find ourselves in dangerous places—physically, spiritually, geographically, financially, relationally, and emotionally. Of these, the most dangerous is the spiritual, as we break our abiding fellowship with the Lord during our time of disobedience.

By not waiting on the Lord, we will not be able to experience God's very best. And why would we want anything but God's very best for us? Why would we choose fast food when He wants to give us the four-course cuisine? Although fast food may be delivered and consumed quickly, it will never be as satisfying and as delicious as the four-course cuisine.

Lastly, our impatience and unwillingness to wait on the Lord may very well hurt others—especially those that we love. Our actions may hurt them as they continue to watch us head down paths they know are not the best for us. If you have ever watched a loved one dig themselves into a hole, you know just how painful it can be.

There have been far too many times in my own life when I did not wait on the Lord. In my pain and my pride, I took matters into my own hands. I decided to handle the situation I was facing, whatever it was at that time, in my own way. My way always seemed to turn out just a bit off at best and flat out wrong at its worst. I did more harm than good, and the consequences of my actions brought additional pain into my life and the lives of those around me. However, every time I trusted and waited on the Lord, no matter how painful the situation or how long it took, God's way was always the best.

So here I am today, choosing a far better option…to wait for the Lord, as He has asked me to do. I want to see the end of the story that He has written. I know what the stories look like that I have written, and they haven't seemed to result in the endings that danced around in my dreams. Too often, it's been more like reading a book in Book Club and at the end of the book saying, "Really? That was the ending? That was awful!"

Yes, for once, I am waiting for God to finish this story. I know from biblical history what happens when people wait on the Lord... they are blessed abundantly. I will wait for that abundant blessing. I will wait on His ending because it's the obedient thing to do, the right thing to do, and because I know His ending will be better than mine ever could be. I will trust the Master Storyteller with my life, watch Him work, and then reap the rewards and blessings of waiting on His perfect storybook ending. (Although I might check my watch once or twice along the way.)

Chapter 6

How We Should Wait

How should we wait? It seems like such a simple question, but the way that we wait reveals the extent to which we trust the One we are ultimately waiting for. So, let's look at ways we can wait that bring glory to the King and help us make it from one day to the next.

Clinging to God

During our waiting time, we need to cling to God. I don't just mean hold on tight until the rough ride is over. I mean that we need to cling to God in a way that we never have before. In our past, we may have clung to other people, to our job, to our hobbies, or to a host of other things. But now, we need to cling to God like our lives depend on it, as in many ways they do.

Jacob is our model for clinging to God and simply not being willing to let go. In Genesis 32, Jacob wrestled with a man until daybreak. He clung to the man until the man said, "'Let me go, for it is daybreak.' But Jacob replied, 'I will not let you go unless you bless me.'"[207] It is believed that Jacob was wrestling with God Himself, and when he simply refused to let go and persistently clung to God, God rewarded that persistence with great blessings.

We, too, will win our victories, not by clinging to our own desires and expectations of what we want our lives to be, but rather by clinging to God in faith. The Lord knows that my life is nothing like I ever planned it would be, and I would bet that many of you would feel the same. And yet, our lives can be far more than we ever thought they could be when we open the doors of our hearts to the Lord and let Him work and bless in ways that we never imagined.

Calling on the Name of the Lord

During our time of waiting, we need to call on the name of the Lord. I am embarrassed to admit that too often, He is not my first "call." On the contrary, it is far more often my mom or dad, my sister or brother, a friend, or someone I think will be sympathetic to my plight or who will provide me with a little bit of encouragement. And then I finally get around to calling on God.

Joel 2:32 reminds us that "everyone who calls on the name of the Lord will be saved."[208] So why don't I call on His name? Why do I run to everyone but Him? Do I think He is just too busy? Or I am just so prideful that I would rather plot out my own course and make my own plans than listen to what He might have in store for me? (That last question hit a little too close to home!)

Regardless of the why, the best place for me to turn is to Him and His loving arms. The best person for me to call is Him because He is *never* too busy for me, He is *always* there, and He *always* has the right answer. I need to stop looking in vain for deliverance from anyone or anything and turn to the Great Deliverer. For He alone has promised that when I turn to Him, I will be saved.

We often don't know when our time of waiting will come to an end. We don't know how much harder the journey will be. But we do know the One who does, and He has literally asked us to call on His name. So, when we feel we can't make it one more step, we need to call on His name and humbly ask Him to save us and carry us the rest of the way.

Depending on God

Our waiting time could not be a better time to depend on God completely and totally. I do not say this lightly because this is not one of my strengths. In all honesty, it's probably one of my more glaring weaknesses. I have always been extremely independent and take great pride in being able to take care of myself. Some very difficult and heart-shattering situations in my own life have resulted in that independence becoming even more deeply ingrained.

Now the world sees this as a great strength, and to an extent, I do too. My own independent nature and ability to take care of myself can be a very good thing if kept in the right balance and context. But when I get my feelings hurt, I can be quick to shut others out and revert to the mindset that no one can take care of me like I can.

The reality is that this is simply not true and one of Satan's many lies that he would like me to believe. During my waiting period, I have had enough broken toilets in my house to know that I need my dad or someone to help me out before I literally start swimming! (And who says God doesn't have a sense of humor?) I have had enough "life" questions that I needed to run by my mom or a good friend to know that without their advice, I would have undoubtedly ended up on an episode of Dr. Phil (or Jerry Springer). I have had enough times of being alone where I recognized that I need a family and friends to share my life with—through the good times and the bad.

Feeling completely self-sufficient, to the exclusion of God, family, an intimate loved one, or friends, is not where God wants us to be. He has used my own time of waiting to make me ever more mindful of that and ever more dependent on Him. Undoubtedly, I will need to be weary of heading back into Independence Land—especially when someone says or does something to hurt my heart—but at least I know that is the Land to which I tend to quickly retreat.

You may be just like me in this respect. Just remember, we can depend on God. He won't let us down. Others have let us down, others currently are letting us down, and others will let us down in the future, but He will not. They may not mean to, but they are just as human and prone to mistakes as we are.

So, when we hit those hard times of waiting, instead of asking ourselves, "What can I do?" why don't we step back and ask, "Lord, what can you do in this situation? What miracle can You work?

What immovable mountain can You move?" I guarantee, whatever we thought we could do on our own, will pale in comparison to what the Great Doer can accomplish if we will only just depend on Him.

Being Honest with God

If I have learned nothing else during this time of waiting, I have learned that I must wait honestly. What I mean by that is that I must honestly, and without reservation, empty out my heart to the Lord. I must tell Him what I am feeling and what I am thinking. I must tell Him when my heart feels like it is literally breaking into a million pieces. I must tell Him how much I appreciate the things He does to encourage me and uses to light my way during my time of waiting. I need to tell Him when I no longer have a clue how to pray because I have been praying for so long about the same exact thing that it seems I have run out of things to say. And I need to tell Him when I just don't think I can make it one more day.

We all need to take a lesson from David on honestly speaking our hearts to the Lord. God called David "a man after his own heart,"[209] and I believe that part of that was because David was so completely honest and transparent with the Lord about everything he was feeling. From the lowest of lows to the highest of highs, David opened his full heart to the Lord.

In the middle of one of his lowest lows, David, full of despair, wrote Psalm 13:1-2:

> How long, O Lord? Will You forget me forever?
> How long will You hide Your face from me?
> How long must I wrestle with my thoughts
> And day after day have sorrow in my heart?
> How long will my enemy triumph over me?[210]

And yet, in the same breath, David also praised God's unfailing love in Psalm 13:5-6:

> But I trust in Your unfailing love;
> My heart rejoices in Your salvation.
> I will sing the Lord's praise,
> For He has been good to me.[211]

David experienced many emotional mountains and valleys in his life, and yet he freely laid them before the Lord. He chose to be completely vulnerable and real with the God of the Universe. In that spirit of being honest, we honestly need to do the same with God.

The funny thing is that God already knows exactly what's on our minds and hearts. In fact, He knew exactly what we would think and exactly what we would feel at this very moment and every moment in our lives before time even began. Kind of crazy to think about, isn't it? So, our thoughts—however wretched and embarrassing and lacking in spirituality we may find them to be—are no surprise to God.

So, speak up. Tell Him when you are disappointed with His timetable of bringing promises to fruition. It's okay. He already knows, and laying our hearts bare before the Lord, just like David did, can be rather healing. It allows God to go to work on some of the beautiful parts of our lives that we are proud of, as well as the parts that we would rather see buried forever.

As I write this, I am laughing at the memory of a moment of total honesty with the Lord that landed on the "let's bury it forever" side. After sitting through a great Sunday morning service at my church, I was feeling spiritually invigorated. As I was leaving the church, I walked past a woman who was walking in with her husband, looking as happy as she could be. I took a second look at her and in my head said, "Lord, really? How in the world does *she* have a man and I don't?" Not being one of my better moments, I literally stopped in my tracks, horrified at the thought that had run through my head and that I hoped had run itself straight to China. Still, at a complete stop on the church sidewalk, the next thought that ran through my head was, "Well, since I obviously learned nothing in the last service, I might as well head right back into the next church service for Round Two."

I didn't go back in for Round Two, but I did finally get moving off the church sidewalk. The bottom line is this: it wasn't one of my prouder moments, but I was proud of my honesty with the Lord and with myself. And I truly believe our gracious Heavenly Father is just as proud of us when we are honest, albeit painfully honest, with Him.

Fixing Our Eyes on God

It can be so easy, as we wait, to become focused upon our seemingly insurmountable circumstances rather than the supernatural power of our God. Even the disciples, the men that spent more time alone with Jesus than any other group of human beings, at times focused on the wrong things.

Peter gives us a perfect example of what not to focus on in Matthew 14:22-32. In this Bible story, He sees Jesus walking across the water to the boat that he and the other disciples are in. They are all scared to death, thinking they are seeing a ghost. Peter bravely calls out, "Lord, if it's You...tell me to come to You on the water."[212] It is Jesus, and He does tell Peter to come. "Then Peter got down out of the boat, walked on the water and came toward Jesus. But when he saw the wind, he was afraid and, beginning to sink, cried out, 'Lord, save me!'"[213]

Now, we should give Peter some credit here, as he was the only one of the disciples who had the faith and courage to get out of the boat in the first place. But Peter, like many of us, started looking around him. The wind that had been buffeting the boat was now stirring up the doubt in his soul—the very natural human doubt—and he quickly began to sink. He was petrified, and the more petrified he became, the more he took his eyes off the One who could save him. It was like his own fear became the lead weight that Satan was going to use to sink him to the bottom of the lake.

Let's stop here for just a second. We know that Jesus did not tell Peter to get out of the boat and come to Him just so He could allow Satan to use Peter's fear to drown him in front of the other disciples. Where would the victory be in that? It might have even meant the attrition of a few disciples who decided they wanted no part of this mess.

No, Jesus called Peter out of the boat, so He could teach us all a lesson about where to fix our eyes. You see, Peter's biggest mistake occurred when he took his eyes off Jesus. When his eyes were glued to His Master—the environment, the wind, and the other disciples—all ceased to exist. But when he started to look around, the enormity of what he was doing hit him—he was walking on water—and the cement shoes of doubt started to turn his miracle into his worst nightmare.

God knows how overwhelming our circumstances can be, and how like Peter, the cement shoes of doubt can start to sink us. That's why repeatedly, the Bible admonishes us to fix our eyes on God. Proverbs 4:25 says, "Let your eyes look straight ahead, fix your gaze directly before you."[214] Looking straight ahead means that we take our eyes off of our circumstances and we stop looking around at the what-ifs.

Psalm 123:1 says, "I lift up my eyes to You, to You who sit enthroned in heaven."[215] We need to lift our eyes up and away from our circumstances and our waiting to the King of Heaven and Earth. Psalm 141:8 says, "But my eyes are fixed on You Sovereign Lord."[216] Our eyes need to be fixed on the Sovereign Lord, not turning to the right or the left.

And Hebrews 12:2 encourages us by saying, "Let us fix our eyes on Jesus, the pioneer and perfecter of our faith."[217] Fixing our eyes on Jesus takes faith and a great deal of faith at that. It requires faith because we have to take our eyes off our past, present, and future and fix our eyes on Jesus. This is where Peter was tripped up. His faith faltered because he focused on his present situation, albeit a terrifying and life-threatening one.

Perhaps we take our eyes off the Lord in a different manner than Peter. Perhaps rather than looking all around us at the present circumstances that threaten to overwhelm us, we tend to look behind us at our past. We strain our necks around to see what we left in our wake. I believe that's exactly why Paul wrote in Philippians 3:12-14, "Not that I have already obtained all this, or have already arrived at my goal, but I press on to take hold of that for which Christ Jesus took hold of me. Brothers and sisters, I do not consider myself yet to have taken hold of it. But one thing I do: Forgetting what is behind and straining toward what is ahead, I press on toward the goal to win the prize for which God has called me heavenward in Christ Jesus."[218]

Using the analogy of a runner (or a walker if running isn't your thing), if we continue to look back over our shoulders at what's behind us, we are: 1. Losing sight of the very goal of our race—the finish line; 2. Putting ourselves in danger as we come across obstacles in our paths which we cannot see because we are looking backward; 3. Placing more importance on what is behind us than the precious blessings God has in store for us in the future. Why would we do that?

We do that because we get scared. Even when we know that what was behind us wasn't any good for us or may have even been destroying us, we knew what to expect. Although it may have been a terrible situation, we had a certain comfort level of knowing just how bad the bad really was. When we fix our eyes on God and go forward into the future, we have no idea what to expect. The only thing we can expect is the unexpected, and that can be beyond scary.

For the Israelites, braving the scary meant moving forward into the Promised Land. And God has a Promised Land ready and waiting our arrival. We just must fix our eyes on Him and take one step at a time into our future and the destiny that He has awaiting us.

Hoping Expectantly

Waiting and hoping are bound together like the strands of a rope. You see, the definition of "hope" is to desire something with confident expectation of its fulfillment. The definition of "Wait" is to remain or rest in expectation.[219] Both require one being in a state of "expectation" for what is to come. If we didn't believe in the depths of our hearts that something great was coming, then we wouldn't be willing to wait for it. But hope drives us on in our waiting period, beckoning us to hold on one more day, one more hour, and one more minute for God's best for us.

As we wait, we can do so passively, or we can do so hoping expectantly. A passive person is one who hopes something will happen but relinquishes that hope after a short time of that hope being unfulfilled. A person hoping expectantly always believes that the answer is just around the corner. This person wakes up every morning believing that this will be the day God's promises will come to fruition. Then one day, although she may wait and wait for what may seem like forever, that day finally comes.

It's much like when a woman is pregnant; we say that she is expecting a baby. She carries the promise of that baby with her every day. She and her husband eagerly plan for the coming of their baby by getting the nursery ready, collecting all the right supplies, and buying books so they will know how to do this "parenting" thing. And then, one day, their hopeful expectations are met with a beautiful bundle of joy.

Now unlike those of us in waiting, an expectant mother has a pretty good idea of when her baby will be born—approximately forty weeks from the date of conception. We, unfortunately, aren't so lucky. Typically, our waiting comes with no timetable, but that is part of the process. In most cases, we find that this waiting period serves a much greater role in terms of preparing us for the answer that is to come. As Joyce Meyer said, "If God answered right away, many of us would be ill-prepared to handle His solution."

So, we wait in hope for what we do not see and on a timetable that we are not privy to. Painful? Yes. Gut-wrenching? Yes. At times disappointing? Yes, yes, and yes. That's because when we are in our time of waiting, we just can't see what is ahead and when this will all end. And for most of us, seeing is typically the one thing we value the most.

Thankfully, hope is a kind of a vision—a vision of the heart—allowing us to see beyond our current circumstances to what will be. Hope enables us to see what is to come through the eyes of our hearts. Ephesians 1:18-20 captures this perfectly as it says, "I pray that the eyes of your heart may be enlightened in order that you may know the hope to which He has called you, the riches of His glorious inheritance in His holy people, and His incomparably great power for us who believe. That power is the same as the mighty strength He exerted when He raised Christ from the dead and seated Him at his right hand in the heavenly realms."[220]

God has an "incomparably great power for us who believe." So, as we continue to wait for all that we are hoping for, our real hope needs to be focused on God Himself. He is the One who has the power to change our circumstances, to bring to fruition the desires of our hearts, to bring our waiting to an end. I believe that's why so many verses in Scripture talk about hoping in Him.

In Psalm 39:7, David says, "But now, Lord, what do I look for? My hope is in You."[221] Psalm 33:22 also says, "May your unfailing love be with us, Lord, even as we put our hope in You."[222] Psalm 42:11 again echoes something so similar in, "Put your hope in God."[223] Why do all of these verses encourage us to put our hope in Him? *He will never fail us.* Situations will. People will. He will *not*.

We are also told to put our hope in His Word. Psalm 119:114 says, "You are my refuge and my shield; I have put my hope in Your word."[224] And Psalm 130:5 echoes the same thing as it says, "I wait for the LORD, my whole being waits, and in his word I put my hope."[225] So, why do we get that direction? We get that direction because God's word is unbreakable. He can never lie. So, what He has promised will be done. Period.

We also know that "His compassions never fail," and He has an "unfailing love" for us.[226] He wouldn't bring us this far to dash our dreams. He wouldn't bring us this far to sink our ships of hope. He just loves us too much to do that.

That's why He even tells us how to wait in hope. Romans 12:12 encourages us to "Be joyful in hope, patient in affliction, faithful in prayer."[227] Hebrews 6:11-12 goes on to encourage us, saying, "We want each of you to show this same diligence to the very end, so that what you hope for may be fully realized. We do not want you to become lazy, but to imitate those who through faith and patience inherit what has been promised."[228] God wants our hope to be fully realized, but for that to happen, we must be diligent until the very end, and we must have patience.

Romans 8:25 carries on that theme of patience as it says, "But if we hope for what we do not yet have, we eagerly wait for it patiently."[229] Now, how in the world do we reconcile "eagerly" waiting with "patiently" waiting? We excitedly wait for what is to come, but we wait patiently on God's glorious timetable.

It seems so easy to talk of patience and eagerly waiting, but how do we continue to keep our hope buoyed up even amidst the roughest of times? Let's look at Isaiah 40:30-31 in terms of what it promises us when we put our hope in the Lord.

> Even youths grow tired and weary,
> and young men stumble and fall;
> but those who hope in the LORD
> will renew their strength.

They will soar on wings like eagles;
they will run and not grow weary,
they will walk and not be faint.[230]

God's Word tells us that when we put our "hope in the Lord," the only place to put our hope as we have already discussed, He we will renew our strength. Often during our time of waiting, strength is the one thing we have in rather short supply. Waiting is absolutely exhausting emotionally, and the emotional burden seems to sap our physical strength as well. But we are told that God will renew our strength, and if we look at the passage, we see an interesting scale from high energy to low energy. The verses move from "soar" to "run" to "walk." Nothing in the Bible is done without purpose, and I believe God had a specific purpose in the way He moved us down the "energy" scale here.

The reality is that in our waiting period, God knows there will be some days where the emotional burden is low, and on those days, we seem to soar. Other days, the emotional pain is a little heavier and we aren't quite soaring, but at least we are still running. And then there are those days where the emotional burden is so heavy, running is out of the question, and we find ourselves doing our best to manage a walk. I am surprised there wasn't a line in this verse about crawling, as I am sure we can all attest to having those days as well.

God will give us the exact amount of strength we need for the emotional place in which our hearts reside. From soaring to walking, He knows there will be good days and bad days. He just wants us to put our hope in the one place we will never find disappointment— Him.

Perhaps even more difficult a question is where does our hope originate from when it literally begins to run out? Where do we get more hope when our hearts are so badly bruised during our waiting? The Scriptures are very specific in answering this question as we see in Psalm 62:5, "Yes, my soul, find rest in God; my hope *comes from Him*."[231] Second Thessalonians 2:16-17 emphasizes this again by saying, "May our Lord Jesus Christ Himself and God our Father, who loved us and by His grace *gave us* eternal encouragement and good hope, encourage your hearts and strengthen you in every good deed and word."[232]

Romans 15:13 continues to drive the point home as it states, "May the God of hope fill you with all joy and peace as you trust in Him, so that you may overflow with hope by the power of the Holy Spirit."[233] But in this verse, we are not just told that hope comes from Him or that He gave us good hope, but rather that He is the "God of hope" and that as we "trust in Him," we will "overflow with hope" through the "power of the Holy Spirit." Can someone give me an Amen? I mean overflowing with hope? There are some days I am lucky I have a teeny itty-bitty drop in the bottom of my worn-out heart, much less an overflowing amount.

When we dive into God's promises regarding hope, it is hard not to start to feel our worn-out hearts filling up with the hope of what the future will hold. I hate to give away the ending of the story, but Jeremiah 29:11 tells us, "For I know the plans I have for you," declares the Lord, "plans to prosper you and not to harm you, plans to give you hope and a future."[234] God has awesome plans for us and for our futures that will build on the hope we already have for what is to come.

Proverbs 23:18 echoes that as it says, "There is surely a future hope for you, and your hope will not be cut off."[235] Why won't our hope be cut off? Because Hebrews 10:23 reminds us that "He who promised is faithful."[236]

As if His faithfulness wasn't enough, Lamentations 3:25 states, "The Lord is good to those whose hope is in Him, to the one who seeks Him."[237] As we dig into the Scriptures even further, we find that God doesn't just want to be "good to those whose hope is in Him." According to 1 Timothy 6:17, those of us who "put their hope in

God" will be met with God providing "us with everything for our enjoyment."[238] God longs to be good to us as a loving father would long to be good to his children. He just happens to have a few more resources at His command.

Beyond God just being good to us and providing things for our enjoyment, our time of waiting and hoping expectantly is guaranteed to produce in us perseverance, character, and a deeper hope. Romans 5:3-5 says, "Not only so, but we also glory in our sufferings, because we know that suffering produces perseverance; perseverance, character; and character, hope. And hope does not put us to shame, because God's love has been poured out into our hearts through the Holy Spirit, whom He has given us."[239]

Once again, we should recognize that God's progression from suffering to perseverance to character to hope was not accidental. Suffering produces perseverance because it is far easier to quit than to keep going when times are difficult. Perseverance produces character because it takes character to continue to hope day in and day out with no signs of deliverance. Character produces hope because the deeper our character becomes, the more we come to know and love God, and the more we place our hope in the Giver of Hope.

God knows that we are faithfully waiting with hopeful expectation for what is around the corner. He will not be late, and when He finally unlatches the gate to our future, we will find our expectations simply blown away. I believe the following poem captures this just beautifully:

> Waiting! Yes, patiently waiting?
> Till next made plain will be;
> To hear, with the inner hearing,
> The Voice that will call for me.
>
> Waiting! Yes, hopefully waiting?
> With hope that need not grow dim;

The Master is pledged to guide me,
And my eyes are unto Him.

Waiting! Expectantly waiting!
Perhaps it may be today
The Master will quickly open
The gate to my future way.

Waiting! Yes, waiting! Still waiting!
I know, though I've waited long,
That, while He withholds His purpose,
His waiting cannot be wrong.

Waiting! Yes, waiting! Still waiting!
The Master will not be late:
Since He knows that I am waiting
For Him to unlatch the gate.[240]

So, don't surrender your hope...victory is close by.

Letting God Lead

One of the best things we can do as we wait is to let God lead. I took dance lessons years ago, and I must admit that it was an interesting life lesson. It seemed the individual I had been paired up with, and I just couldn't seem to get in synch. I had been told I have good rhythm (and not just by family members!), so I didn't think that was the problem. But it wasn't clear to me what the problem was until I had the chance to dance with the instructor. He was a wonderful dancer, and I naturally let him lead me—pushing and pulling me where he wanted me to go. I trusted him and his abilities and knew he would lead me in the right direction.

Our waiting period is much like a dance floor with our partner being Jesus. He is the most trustworthy partner we could ever wish for. As we dance with Him, we need to completely let go and let Him lead. If we continually struggle to hand over control or to take over control, then we will find ourselves baffled and disappointed at the result.

As Margaret Feinberg so beautifully puts it, "My calling is to press my face into the shoulder blades of Jesus so that wherever He leads I will go." We need to press into the shoulder blades of Jesus, losing ourselves in the moment and trusting Him utterly and completely. When we press in that tightly, we gain a new sense of strength and purpose. His love literally radiates through us. And we become so intoxicated by His love that you don't want to lose a single second being enveloped in His nearness. As we press into Him, the direction of our steps becomes far less relevant to us than knowing the One who is guiding those steps.

The beautiful thing is that God wants to lead us today on the dance floor of our waiting, as well as into the future where amazing blessings will spring forth. In fact, in Psalm 119:105, the psalmist writes, "Your word is a lamp for my feet, a light on my path."[241] This is such a wonderful metaphor because when you think about it, a "lamp for my feet" represents God's guiding us in the here and now. His lamp is lighting the way for each step we need to take today. His "light on my path" can be seen as God's guiding us for the future. God very rarely allows us to see much of the path because if He did, we might all go running in the opposite direction. But He knows what lies ahead, and His light will safely lead us through it.

So, let Him lead. Press in tightly. And enjoy the beauty of the dance.

Loving God

During our time of waiting, the most important lesson we can learn is how to love God. It is so easy to love the Lord when He has "done great things for us."[242] "[W]e are filled with joy" and everything seems right with the world.[243]

But God doesn't just want our love when His gifts and blessings are flowing in our direction. He wants far more than that. He wants a relationship with us that supersedes the giving of gifts. He wants a relationship with us that goes deeper than us just holding our hands out, waiting for the next blessing. He wants a relationship with us that will weather the ups and downs of life and is based on the knowledge that we love Him and want His love more than even the things for which we wait.

Praising God

We are called to praise God in our time of waiting. Psalm 134:1-2 says, "Praise the LORD, all you servants of the LORD who minister by night in the house of the LORD. Lift up your hands in the sanctuary and praise the LORD."[244] "You may see this as a strange time to worship—'minister[ing] by night in the house of the Lord.' Indeed, worshipping at night, during the depth of our sorrows, is a difficult thing. Yet therein lies the blessing, for it is the test of perfect faith."[245]

In our time of waiting, when we are in so much pain, saying we should be "praising God" is a lot like pouring lemon juice on a cut. But we aren't being asked to praise God for the pain we are in or the despair we are feeling. We are being asked to praise God for who He is and what He is teaching us.

Every time my siblings and I have gone through a tough time— whether it was a sports injury, a tough relationship, or just life hitting us hard—my mom would always ask if we had thanked God for the trial. Now, as you can imagine, we had various reactions to that question depending on the depth of our disappointment or hurt at the time. Not all those reactions would have made the "things are parents are so proud of" list.

Looking back, though, my mom wasn't asking us to be thankful for the hurt and disappointment that the trial had brought into our lives. I mean, some of these trials were life-altering. But she was asking us to be thankful for His love and what He would teach us through the trial.

The writer of Psalm 103:2-13 understood this. Listen to His words as he praises God for who He is:

> Praise the LORD, my soul,
> and forget not all His benefits—
> who forgives all your sins
> and heals all your diseases, who redeems your life from the pit
> and crowns you with love and compassion,
> who satisfies your desires with good things
> so that your youth is renewed like the eagle's.
> The LORD works righteousness
> and justice for all the oppressed.
> He made known His ways to Moses,
> His deeds to the people of Israel:
> The LORD is compassionate and gracious,
> slow to anger, abounding in love.
> He will not always accuse,
> nor will He harbor his anger forever;
> He does not treat us as our sins deserve
> or repay us according to our iniquities.
> For as high as the heavens are above the earth,
> so great is His love for those who fear Him;
> as far as the east is from the west,
> so far has He removed our transgressions from us.
> As a father has compassion on His children,
> so the LORD has compassion on those who fear Him.[246]

It is hard not to praise God when you look at this list—forgiver of sins, healer of diseases, redeemer of life, lover of our souls, compassionate one, satisfier of desires, giver of righteousness and justice, gracious one, and merciful one.

He is to be praised for who He is, and if we, by chance, forget everything that He has done for us in our day-to-day living, then we need simply to look at the cross. For it is there He paid the ultimate price of love for us. He loved us enough to give all that He had so that we would have life eternal with Him. I would say that falls into the praiseworthy category.

It is so easy to praise God when we just got a promotion, when we are blessed with a beautiful new baby, or when our spouse is treating us like gold. The question is, what do we do in the hard times? Are we fair-weather praise-givers? Do our praises only come out when the sun is shining, there isn't a cloud in the sky, and the bluebirds are singing?

Unfortunately, the answer for far too many of us is yes. Now, it is wonderful to praise God when good things come our way as He is the Giver of all blessings. But we need to make sure that we praise Him on both sides of our circumstances—the good and the bad.

The Israelites provide a great example of praising God, but just doing so on the "good" side of their Red Sea circumstance. God had brought them out of bondage, and they were headed to the Promised Land. Unfortunately, Pharaoh had a change of heart and came charging after them. Rather than praising God for whom He was and all that He had already done, the Israelites threw a bit of a temper tantrum.

In fact, Exodus 14:10-12 says,

> As Pharaoh approached, the Israelites looked up, and there were the Egyptians, marching after them. They were terrified and cried out to the Lord. They said to Moses, "Was it because there were no graves in Egypt that you brought us to the desert to die? What have you done to us by bringing us out of Egypt? Didn't we say to you in Egypt, 'Leave us alone; let us serve the Egyptians'? It would have been better for us to serve the Egyptians than to die in the desert."[247]

They were deathly afraid as it appeared their two options were death by Egyptians or death by drowning. God had just delivered them from Pharaoh's bondage through a series of miracles, and yet that seemed to have slipped their minds. And He had not worked out miracle after miracle to take them to the edge of the Red Sea to die. So, He worked another miracle, parted the Red Sea, and they walked through on dry land. Pharaoh's army was swallowed up by the sea, and then the Israelites rejoiced and sang songs of praise.

It's a wonderful story until you realize that the Israelites rejoiced on the wrong side of the Red Sea. And too often, that's exactly what we do. Once God has delivered us from our waiting, we will sing and praise and rejoice. But we need to learn to sing on the right side of our "waiting sea." We may not see His plan or His deliverance clearly, but we need to learn to praise God on the right side of our waiting.

I want it to be said of me that when my trial of waiting was over, I praised God on both sides of the waiting period. I am sure you do too. The beauty of it is that when we are praising God, our problems fade into the background and our hurts seem to dissolve even if for but a brief time. I guess it's hard to stay focused on ourselves and our difficult circumstances when our hands are lifted high in praise to the Lover of our souls.

Praying Faithfully

During our waiting time, prayer is the link that connects us back to God and to His endless power. It's our supernatural weapon in our time of greatest need. God even directs us to come to Him with holy boldness and divine confidence, for He is looking not for great people but for people who will dare to prove the greatness of their God!

Our prayers are God's opportunity to demonstrate that greatness. So, we must beware of limiting God to what we humanly think is possible or by thinking we know exactly what He may do. We should learn to expect the unexpected. Isaiah 64:4 reminds us, "no one has heard, no ear has perceived, no eye has seen any God besides you, who acts on behalf of those who wait for Him."[248]

As we continue to pray faithfully for the unexpected, we need to have confident trust that God will do what we have asked for. Why should we have that confident trust? God, Himself, tells us to have that confidence in Him and His ability to answer our prayers. Mark 11:24 says, "Therefore I tell you, whatever you ask for in prayer, believe that you have received it, and it will be yours."[249] In John 14:13, Jesus Himself says, "And I will do whatever you ask in My name, so that the Father may be glorified in the Son."[250] Again, in John 16:23, Jesus says, "My Father will give you whatever you ask in My name."[251]

We need to respond in a manner worthy of God's direction, and that includes behaving as if He has already granted our request. This attitude includes leaning upon Him and trusting that what we have prayed for, we will one day claim. As this lovely little poem sums up,

The thing I ask when God leads me to pray,
Begins in the same act to come my way.[252]

In my own life, one of my periods of waiting included waiting for the man God would bring into my life as my spouse. This one made my daily prayer list, as well as those of many precious friends and family. Then one day, God called me to buy a dresser to match my current bedroom set. Now, to make this perfectly clear, I was *very* single at the time and had been so for a long period of time. As the Lord laid this on my heart, I literally looked around my bedroom and said, "Do you see something I don't, Lord? As of right now, I have plenty of furniture in my bedroom." Then I felt the Lord say to me, "It's not for you. It's for your future husband."

Well, it's kind of tough to argue with that kind of direction, although no man was in sight. That very weekend I faithfully headed down to my favorite furniture store to find a dresser to match my bedroom set. Now, I had owned my master bedroom set for several years. The possibility of finding a dresser to exactly match my set was slim to none, and I was banking on none. But then again, the odds seem to change when there is supernatural power involved.

Not only did the very first dresser I set eyes on exactly match my set, but it was on sale! You gotta love a bargain, and personally I took that as confirmation that the Lord is a bargain shopper as well. The salesman who had been assisting me began filling out my paperwork and kindly asked me if I was buying this for my husband. I smiled at him with teary eyes and said, "Why yes, I am."

That dresser has become my own "Noah's ark." Thankfully God did not call me to build the dresser because He omnisciently knew that I am *no* carpenter. But He did tell me to buy my "Noah's ark" as a reminder of the promise He made to me for my future husband.

So, as we build or buy our arks and have confident trust God will do what we have asked for, we naturally come to a tough question. Are there conditions on what He will do? Yes, of course, because if there weren't, we might all ask to have cellulite-free bodies and metabolisms that allowed us to eat an endless supply of chocolate every day. At least I would.

The condition is that we must be walking with the Lord, and therefore, have oneness with Him and His will. John 15:7 says, "If you remain in Me and My words remain in you, ask whatever you wish, and it will be done for you."[253] First John 5:14-15 reinforces this by saying, "This is the confidence we have in approaching God: that if we ask anything according to His will, He hears us. And if we know that He hears us—whatever we ask—we know that we have what we asked of Him."[254]

Genesis 24 provides a beautiful confirmation of asking for something in God's will and receiving it before the prayer itself is even finished. In this story, Abraham asked his servant to help find a wife for his son Isaac, and the servant agreed. On his journey, the servant prayed specifically to the Lord, "May it be that when I say to a young woman, 'Please let down your jar that I may have a drink,' and she says, 'Drink, and I'll water your camels too'—let her be the one you have chosen for your servant Isaac."[255] Talk about praying in specifics! Genesis 24:15 tells us, "Before he had finished praying, Rebekah came out with her jar on her shoulder" and almost word for word repeated back to the servant his prayer to the Lord.[256]

Abraham's servant was very blessed in such an immediate answer to his prayer. We aren't all afforded the same luxury, especially those of us in a season of waiting. Unfortunately, even when we have prayed in total and complete faith, the interim between asking and receiving is one of the most trying times we may ever face. Rather than God responding immediately to our prayers, we are called to wait for what seems like an eternity. Rather than rising from our praying knees and with total joy finding the answer to our prayers ringing the doorbell, we find that doubt is the one ringing our doorbell.

We may even find ourselves coming to the point in this interim between asking and receiving that we simply don't know how to pray or what to pray for anymore. Romans 8:26-27 tells us, "In the same way, the Spirit helps us in our weakness. We do not know what we ought to pray for, but the Spirit Himself intercedes for us through wordless groans. And He who searches our hearts knows the mind of the Spirit because the Spirit intercedes for God's people in accordance with the will of God."[257] Yes, at times, we may have been praying for so long in our waiting that we don't even know exactly how to word our prayers or express our deepest sorrows. But the Spirit does and will intercede for us, with groans that cannot even be expressed through words.

"So we can simply pour from the fullness of our heart the burden of our spirit and the sorrow that seems to crush us. We can know that He hears, loves, understands, receives, and separates from our prayers everything that is in error, imperfect, or wrong. And then He presents the remainder, along with the incense of the great High Priest, before His throne on high. We may be assured that our prayer is heard, accepted, and answered in His name."

"[W]hen troubled with burdens and difficulties too complicated to put into words and too puzzling to express or fully understand how sweet it is to fall into the embrace of His blessed arms and to simply sob out the sorrow that we cannot speak."[258] The Lord knows how to interpret our very sorrows...even when we do not. However, we utter our prayers in our time of waiting, whether through words or through the groans of our sorrows, we must continue praying faithfully to the One who is ever faithful.

Another hard thing we encounter as we continue to pray faithfully and wait and wait and wait is that we start to feel like our prayers are pointless. Our emotions begin to take over, and the questions abound: if God hasn't answered my prayers yet, is He really going to? Jesus answers that question very clearly—continue to ask, seek, and knock. Matthew 7:7 says, "Ask and it will be given to you; seek and you will find; knock and the door will be opened to you."[259] He is specifically calling us *not* to give up. In fact, in Luke 18:1, we are told that "Jesus told His disciples a parable to show them that they should always pray and not give up."[260]

Not only are we called *not* to give up, but we are also called to pray without ceasing. First Thessalonians 5:17 says, "Pray without ceasing."[261] Rather to the point, right? Again, here is where I wish God gave us an asterisk with this verse that gave us a specific timeline, but He didn't. He wants us to keep praying without ceasing until the prayer has been fulfilled. No ifs, ands, or buts.

Why does He call us to do this? In the first place, if we are praying, we are far less likely to worry about our current situation. We move our eyes off our situations that so quickly drag us down and onto the Lord, who is the only One who can bring our waiting to an end.

In the second place, we see that delayed answers to our prayers are trials of faith used to grow us into more mature Christians. Delays are not refusals of our prayers, but rather evidence that God has a fixed time and ordained purpose for everything in our lives—especially the things for which we wait. So, we let the delays teach us how to be ever more steadfast and persistent in our prayers, letting each prayer build upon the last until we are triumphant.

By the way, the impossibility of our situation means absolutely nothing to the Lord, so we can't use that as an excuse to give up our praying. God loves to bring answers when all we see are obstacles. Can anyone say, "Red Sea"? He is looking at our situation through omnipotent, omniscient eyes while we see them only through human eyes. The impossible situations we are praying for faithfully represent the perfect time for God to do His work.

And the best time for Him to do His work is when we have done everything humanly feasible to solve our problems or change our situation of waiting, and there is still no change. In fact, too often in my own life, I have believed that after I prayed, it was then my responsibility to do everything I possibly could do to help the answer along. "Yet God taught me a better way and showed me that self-effort always hinders His work. He also revealed that when I prayed and had a confident trust in Him for something, He simply wanted me to wait in an attitude of praise and do only what He told me."[262]

The answers I seek won't be a result of my actions, and neither will yours. Our big problems require big answers, and that thankfully is God's specialty. In Mark 10:27, "Jesus looked at them and said, 'With man this is impossible, but not with God; all things are possible with God.'"[263]

Praying faithfully is not easy, but it's the only way to endure our time of waiting. And to pray faithfully, we must:

- Pray without limiting God

- Pray with confident trust

- Pray even when we don't know what to say

- Pray without ceasing.

141

And when "by prayer and petition, with thanksgiving" we present our "requests to God," the peace of God, which transcends all understanding, will guard your hearts and your minds in Christ Jesus.[264] God will answer, and He will do so at just the right time and in just the right way.

Seeking God

One of the best things about the waiting period is that it often gives us ample time to seek God. Although it may seem obvious as to why we should seek Him, I think it would be beneficial to examine the "why" a little more closely. Thankfully, knowing our curious minds, God has already answered that question in such a beautifully simplistic way. It is a lovely process that goes like this: We should seek Him because He asked us to, and doing so is demonstrating obedience; when we seek Him, we will find Him; and He rewards those who seek Him.

We should seek God because He told us to, and doing so is demonstrating obedience. First Chronicles 16:11 says, "Look to the Lord and His strength; seek His face always."[265] First Chronicles 22:19 says, "Now devote your heart and soul to seeking the Lord your God."[266] These verses are directions to us to seek the Lord with our hearts and souls. David himself obeyed these directions and wrote, "You, God, are my God, earnestly I seek you; I thirst for You, my whole being longs for You, in a dry and parched land where there is no water."[267]

But the Lord does not simply issue commands for the sake of issuing them. He asks us to seek Him because when we seek Him, we will find Him. When we seek Him, we will find the very God of the Universe. Deuteronomy 4:29 says, "But if from there you seek the Lord your God, you will find Him if you seek Him with all your heart and with all your soul."[268] Jeremiah 29:13 echoes the same sentiment when it says, "You will seek Me and find Me when you seek Me with all your heart."[269] Proverbs 8:17 states it again..."those who seek Me find Me."[270]

This is not a proverbial game of hide-and-seek where we may be seeking someone for hours and come close to finding them. God tells us that when we seek Him with all our hearts and our souls, we will find Him. Period. Done. Game over, and you are an automatic winner of the greatest prize known to man—finding God. It honestly gives me goosebumps. I mean, I am quite competitive, so knowing that I am going to win before I even get started is exciting!

If that wasn't enough of a reward, God tells us that there are other rewards for those who seek Him. Hebrews 11:6 states, "And without faith it is impossible to please God, because anyone who comes to Him must believe that He exists and that He rewards those who earnestly seek Him."[271] He doesn't spell out what those rewards will be because, quite honestly, each of our situations is unique. This is not a one size fits all kind of reward because one size won't fit all.

In Lamentations 3:25, we are told, "The LORD is good to those whose hope is in Him, to the one who seeks Him."[272] Again, we don't know exactly how He is going to be good to us, but we know He is going to be good to us. Over the years, I have found that God's "good" has always been far more amazing than the "best" I could dream up.

God does tell us one very specific thing that we all need to hear in this time of waiting. No matter what, when we are seeking Him, we will *not* be forsaken. As we wait, it is hard to believe that we have not been forgotten. But David writes, "Those who know Your name trust in You, for You, Lord, have never forsaken those who seek You."[273] And why will He never forsake us? Because He came "to seek and to save the lost." He wants us to find Him, and He won't forsake us when we are looking for Him because He was seeking us first. He was the original seeker, and He is not going to forgo the prize for which He was searching.

Then, it begs the question, exactly how do we seek Him? I know of three ways to seek Him—a triangle of seeking if you will—through Time in the Word, Time in Prayer, and Time in Meditation. When we are seeking Him, we need to spend Time in the Word. We need to study the Bible, seek answers, understand God's promises and claim those promises as our own. We can do it through group Bible Studies, devotionals, or individual study. One of my all-time favorite devotionals has been *Streams in the Desert* because of the practicality of every single message. But the Lord is far less concerned about what devotional we are using daily and far more concerned about us spending time with Him.

The second part of that triangle is spending Time in Prayer. We need to pray about the burdens on our hearts during this waiting time. We need to pray for wisdom and discernment. We need to pray for strength...and the list goes on and on. But our prayers are far less about a "Want List" and more about just communicating with the Great Communicator. Prayer is about our relationship with Him. It is about talking to Him about what is on our hearts and opening our hearts to hear what He is saying back to us.

The final piece of the triangle of seeking is Time in Meditation. Time in Meditation should be focused on meditating on who God is, what He wants to do through us and in us, and how He wants to accomplish it. I have often found that He will speak to me with that still small voice in my Time in Meditation. Now I must admit that sometimes I wish it wasn't just a still small voice. Sometimes I wish it was a still medium or still loud voice. Perhaps even a foghorn—anything to get my attention. But I think He uses that still small voice because I have to lean in even closer to Him to hear it, and He wants me that close, so He has my full attention.

Regardless of the volume of the voice, we know that He directs us. In Isaiah 30:20-21, we are told, "Whether you turn to the right or to the left, your ears will hear a voice behind you, saying, 'This is the way; walk in it.'"[274] I've learned to listen for that voice, to seek Him, and to know that this time of waiting is about preparing my heart for what is to come once all the waiting is over.

Serving God

Waiting means resting in God's timing, but it doesn't mean sitting on our tushies doing nothing. As hard as it may be, we need to continue to take care of our responsibilities until God brings the waiting period to an end. We simply need to keep living and making an impact on others in any way we can.

I am not suggesting we avoid the pain or ignore the loss; Lord knows I have tried, and my pain will simply not be ignored. I am saying that we should keep putting that pain aside for even just a spell, to serve and rejoice with others. We need to keep acknowledging that God is in control of everything in our lives and stay present in the moments where He has us. Staying present in those moments may mean waiting, hurting, wishing, dreaming, crying, and just taking the hard to take the next step. This is what life is all about.

On an outing with my Dad not too long ago, we had a chance to talk about life in general. And he said to me, "Rachel, one of your greatest strengths is that even when you're hurting, you keep serving other people." I was incredibly humbled and touched by that because I had never seen myself from that perspective. I have only been able to see myself through the hurt, wishing I could do more but sometimes just emotionally unable to.

We will all have those times where we are emotionally unable to give anymore to anyone else because of our own state of heart. At those times, the best thing we can do is just curl up on a couch with our Bibles or a good book and a cup of coffee and rest our weary souls. Or perhaps watch a movie. Or perhaps just journal our thoughts and feelings as a way to release the hurt we sometimes feel. Or my personal favorite, dive into a bag of Hershey's Kisses (of course, only after a vigorous workout)!

When we are emotionally able again, let's love with action while we are waiting on God's action. It can be as simple as calling a friend to go out to coffee because you know she is having a tough time. We can bake or buy some banana nut bread for our new neighbors who just moved in next door. We can get involved in organizations that have tugged on our hearts. Regardless of how, we need to love with action. It often helps us take our eyes off our own pain.

Surrendering to God

It's often in the most difficult times of our lives that we are brought to a place of surrendering completely to God. We have done all that we could, we have tried everything we know to try, and we know of nothing else to do. We come to the place where there is literally nothing else we can do but totally surrender everything to the Lord. It's letting Him know that "all I have and all I am are yours."

As scary as surrender may be for us, it is the only way that we will be able to find out what our true divine destiny is in this life. It is the only way we will know who our soul mate will be, what career will be a perfect fit, and what we were really born to do on this earth. Surrendering is the only way to step into God's perfect will for our lives. And His perfect will for us is the most fulfilling realm that we will ever step into.

I recently heard a great baseball analogy about surrendering to God's perfect will. Surrendering to God and His will for our lives is like stepping out of the dugout onto the baseball field. Sure, from the dugout, everything looks pretty good. The fans cheer, the music blares, the whole atmosphere is simply electric. But it's when we step out onto that field that the electric atmosphere electrifies us as well. As long as we hold on to our own lives, we will always be sitting in the dugout. We will be watching the entire game, but we will never be a part of it. The minute we turn our lives over to the Lord and surrender to what He has in store for us, we walk out on the field, enter the game of life, and become electrified.

However, if surrendering was so easy to do—just stepping out onto the field—then everyone would be doing it. There are often three main barriers that block our total surrender to God: 1. Fear: Can I trust God? 2. Pride: Who is in Control? 3. Result: What's the Result? Fear too often keeps us from surrendering our lives to the Lord because if we are honest, we just aren't quite sure we can trust Him. That gets amplified when we are in a period of waiting where we are hurting tremendously. But as 1 John 4:18 tells us, "There is no fear in love. But perfect love drives out fear."[275] That "perfect love" is predicated on us getting to know God and understanding how much He really loves us. As we gain that understanding, we begin to trust Him, and the easier we find it to surrender our lives to His will.

The second barrier is pride: Who is in control? Surrendering is about giving God full control. We have to put to death our own wants, desires, and plans that we have laid out for our lives. We have to turn over the reins of our lives to Him. That becomes a bit less scary when we consider what John 10:10 says, "I came that they may have life, and have *it* abundantly."[276] A surrendered life is an abundant life.

Thankfully, God gave us examples of amazing biblical characters who surrendered their lives to the Lord and were given life abundantly. Abraham followed God's leading without knowing where it would take him. Hannah waited for God's perfect timing without knowing when. Mary expected a miracle without knowing how. Joseph trusted God's purpose without knowing why circumstances happened the way they did. They stopped trying to manipulate others, force their own agendas, and control the situation. They let go and let God work. Instead of trying harder, they trusted more. And God blessed them in ways they could not have imagined.

The final barrier to surrender is result. What's the result? Many of us have a really hard time completely surrendering our lives to God because we are not sure what the result will be. We are afraid that when we surrender, we will all be called to become missionaries in Africa. True, some of us may be called to do just that, but the reality is that He still needs some missionaries here in our current places of work and in our local neighborhoods.

We may also be afraid that God is going to turn us all into robots to serve Him when we surrender our lives to Him. Surrendering is not about repressing who we are and who He made us to be. God made us with exquisitely unique personalities and particular skill sets for a reason. Why would He want that to go to waste? When we surrender our lives to Him, rather than being diminished, He enhances it. C. S. Lewis observed, "The more we let God take us over, the more truly ourselves we become—because he made us."

And as we let Him "take us over," we find the blessings of surrender in peace, freedom, and power. Job 22:21 says, "Submit to God and be at peace with Him; in this way prosperity will come to you."[277] Surrendering results in a peace in our souls as we stop fighting our current circumstances. We accept God's timing. We accept God's ways. We accept the outcome He has planned. We trust Him and Him alone.

We also find freedom in surrender as we learn to let go and let God. Luke 9:24 tells us, "For whoever wants to save their life will lose it, but whoever loses their life for Me will save it."[278] When we stop holding on so tightly to what we want and hand it over to God, there is a freedom that enters our souls. It's the freedom of knowing that we can fall back into His waiting arms, and He will catch us. Can't you just see Him lovingly looking at us, saying, "I got this. Trust me"?

And finally, surrender gives us power—God's power in our lives. This is where the paradox lies as victory comes through surrendering. Surrendering doesn't weaken us; it strengthens us as we let go of the burden caused by the constant striving to control our own lives and destinies.

The reality is that we will all eventually surrender to something. The question is, what will we surrender to? I want to be surrendered to God. Sometimes that may mean repeatedly putting myself back on the altar of sacrifice. As a living sacrifice, I do tend to try to crawl away!

Surrendering is not easy because it's where our faith is tested. See, anyone can keep "doing." Great faith is exhibited not in the ability to do but in the ability to surrender. And surrendered people are the people that God uses. May we all be the people that God wants to use in this game called life.

Trusting God

Trusting God is literally at the heart of our faith, and it is at the heart of our waiting. If we can't trust Him, then we can't trust anything He has said to us along the way. If we can't trust His promises, then we can't trust His guarantee of our salvation. As those who love Him, we do trust Him and all that He has told us. In fact, we have entrusted Him with our very hearts and souls. That makes "trust" truly the language of the heart.

But have you noticed how trusting God with our hearts and souls is sometimes easier than trusting Him with the everyday situations in our lives? Trusting God and His timing in our waiting periods is not easy, but it is also not something we have had to suffer through alone. The stories of Abraham, Moses, and Joseph quickly remind us that waiting is a universal tool God has used throughout the ages to perfect our trust in Him.

Abraham did not and could not understand *why* God would ask him to sacrifice his son Isaac (how could he possibly understand that?), but he trusted God who had been so faithful to Him. He trusted God when nothing seemed to make sense, and God made his descendants as numerous as the stars.

"Moses could not understand why God would require him to stay forty years in the wilderness, but he also trusted Him. Then he saw when God called him to lead Israel from Egyptian bondage."[279] The time in this wilderness was his time of training and preparation so that he could victoriously face Pharaoh and lead the Israelites out of Egypt.

"Joseph could not understand his brothers' cruelty toward him, the false testimony of a treacherous woman, or the long years of unjust imprisonment, but he trusted God, and finally, he saw His glory in it all."[280] God used all of these trials to prepare Joseph to become the governor of a great land and to prevent widespread starvation across an entire nation.

Each of these men undoubtedly came to the point where they wondered why in the world the different afflictions they faced were permitted to enter their lives. They undoubtedly questioned why God had led them down paths twisting and turning, with what seemed to be no rhyme or reason. They probably even wondered why the plans they thought were so well laid out seemed to lead to nothing but disappointment.

Have you been there? Are you there now? I have been. I don't understand all of God's ways of dealing with us, and to be quite honest, I am rather glad I don't. You see, if I did and my simple brain could grasp what the Creator of the Universe was always doing, well, He might begin to lose a little bit of His mystery. That's why He doesn't expect us to understand everything He is doing. He knows we simply can't. He functions on a different level than we ever will, even on our best days.

I do know, however, that someday we will look back on our periods of waiting, and we will see God's glory in ways we could not imagine at the time. We will see how the pieces fell into place to finish off the puzzle. As we wait, though, our lives seem to look far more like a puzzle that has been strewn across the table than we would care to admit. Some pieces are upside down, and all we can see is their cardboard backing. Some pieces have straight edges, while some have no edges. Some have bright colors, and some are solid black. Some pieces seem to fit perfectly together, and some pieces look like they came from a different puzzle altogether. And some pieces look like they came from a different puzzle altogether.

With puzzles, we can see the picture the manufacturer has given us on the front of the box so we know what our puzzle will look like. And we trust that we were provided all the pieces we need to make that puzzle come to life. In our life puzzle, all we have is the pieces strewn everywhere. We have no final picture, and the box lid is nowhere to be found. But if we can trust a puzzle manufacturer to give us the right pieces to make a beautiful picture, how much more can we trust God? You see, He has already solved the puzzle of our lives, and everything we are going through now is required to make the picture stunning.

Our spiritual forefathers trusted the puzzles of their lives to God. They had a firm belief in the reliability, truth, ability, or strength of God. They had a firm belief in what He promised to do. But should we? Should we trust God?

Again, we look to David, "a man after God's own heart." He first talks about his own trust in God, encourages us to trust God, and then tells us why. He talks of that trust in Psalm 56:3 as he says, "When I am afraid, I put my trust in You."[281] In Psalm 52:8-9, he says, "But I am like an olive tree flourishing in the house of God; I trust in God's unfailing love forever and ever."[282]

David then talks of us trusting God. In Psalm 62:8, he admonishes us, "Trust in Him at all times, you people; pour out your hearts to Him, for God is our refuge."[283] In Psalm 4:5, he tells us to "[o]ffer the sacrifices of righteousness, and trust in the Lord."[284] Psalm 37:3 tells us to "[t]rust in the Lord and do good."[285]

Then we are told why we should trust God, and the list is lengthy. Psalm 9:10 tells us that we should trust God because he has "never forsaken" those who seek Him.[286] Psalm 28:7 talks about trust in the Lord as "my strength and my shield" because "He helps me."[287] Psalm 37:4-6 encourages us by saying, "Take delight in the Lord, and He will give you the desires of your heart. Commit you way to the Lord; trust in him and he will do this: He will make your righteous reward shine like the dawn, your vindication like the noonday sun."[288] "Trust in him"...and "He will make your righteous reward shine like the dawn." Unbelievable, but I think He had me at "reward" shining "like the dawn."

Other Scriptures confirm and expound upon what the psalmists wrote. Isaiah 26:3 says, "You will keep in perfect peace those whose minds are steadfast, because they trust in you."[289] Jeremiah 17:7 tells us, "But blessed is the one who trusts in the Lord, whose confidence is in him."[290]

Looking back at all these verses, we find that trusting God means we will never be forsaken. We will be helped. We will receive a righteous reward. We will have perfect peace. We will be blessed. What a list! But I believe that if we take a deeper look at Scripture overall, we will find that we should trust God not because of this amazing list of promises but because He is deserving of our trust. He is trustworthy, and we know that because not once in all of history did He ever make a promise that He did not deliver on. Not once. *Every promise kept. Every time!*

When we trust God, we are trusting power that literally raised the dead, calmed the seas, and healed the sick. We are trusting power that resurrected a beaten, thorn-crowned, speared Jesus from the dead, and may be moments from rolling our personal stones away.

Our waiting is fundamentally wrapped up with knowing, trusting, and believing in God, His character, His promises, and His power. We must have confidence in God's wisdom, His love, His timing, and His deep understanding of the situation that we are in. Waiting means knowing and trusting God.

But are there times in our lives, especially in our waiting, that we feel trusting God and His promises have brought us to the edge of a cliff? Yes. Do we grow impatient while we wait on God to work? I do. But the time to trust is when the darkest clouds are in the sky, when our prayers seem to be hitting a cement ceiling, when we feel alone, broken, and bruised.

In the times where we struggle, Proverbs 3:5-6 admonishes us, "Trust in the Lord with all your heart and lean not on your own understanding; In all your ways submit to Him, and He will make your paths straight."[291] God revels in our trust and desires to act on our behalf when we trust in Him. But we can't depend on our own understanding of our situation to get us through.

I am sure if Noah honestly assessed his situation as he built the biggest boat the world had ever seen with not a drop of rain in sight, he might have started to question his own sanity. Instead of using his own understanding of the situation he found himself in, he trusted God and God's knowledge of what was to come. Noah submitted his ways to God, and God made a path for him and his family straight into a new world.

Unfortunately, trusting God with our difficult situations is not a decision we make just once. It is far more often a choice that we make hundreds upon hundreds of times, even in the same day with decision after decision. See, trust is not a passive state of attitude or mind. Trust is a dynamic, vital action of the heart and soul in which we take hold of the promises of God and refuse to let go day after day as we wait.

Waiting takes time, it takes trust, and it takes holding on until completion. As we fight on, we often find that the only way out is through...and the only way through is by trusting God. "He led the Israelites to the Red Sea—He's led you to yours. God allowed Daniel to be thrown into a den of lions—He's done the same with you. He gave David the opportunity to defeat a giant—He's giving you the chance as well. He permitted Shadrach, Meshach, and Abednego to step into a fiery furnace, but He met them there—He'll meet you in your furnace of affliction. He gave Peter the opportunity to walk on water—He's calling you upon it too. But you'll have to trust Him. That's what He's after...your trust in Him. He's after your heart...the one that's breaking. And He needs you to decide...sometimes many times a day, hour, or minute—to trust Him. It's your choice—He leaves the decision to you. When we make that decision, Romans 10:11 reminds us, "Anyone who believes in him will never be put to shame."[292]

Although we won't be put to shame, there are times when we feel our waiting beginning to wear thin our trust of God's handling of our situation. It's then that our gracious God will guide us through our circumstances. And He often uses what would appear as trivial incidents to anyone else, but to us, those incidents speak volumes. Those trivial incidents are like little beacons of light encouraging us to continue to sail forward.

I personally had it happen in my own life as at the beginning of my waiting; God laid a promise on my heart. Then throughout my waiting time, He reinforced that promise continuously in what would have appeared to be the most trivial of ways to anyone else. To my eyes of faith, those trivial ways spoke volumes and helped me hang on until the promise was fulfilled.

As we advance toward the time of our promise being fulfilled, waiting means trusting God and continuing to claim His promises. As we trust God, our faith is deepened. As our faith is deepened, we believe in God's ability to work miracles and to do the impossible. As we believe in God's ability to do the impossible, we begin to see that behind this trial of waiting lies something amazing—we just have to trust. God is never late.

Chapter 7

A Precaution While Waiting

I want to offer up one precaution that I had to learn the hard way. During our time of waiting, choose carefully with whom you share your heart. There are some people who "get it." They "get it" because, most likely, they too have been through an enduring and long-lasting period of waiting. They "get it" because they have been through the darkness, the pain, and the suffering and have come out on the other side. Those people will respond with love, compassion, empathy, and encouragement. You walk away from conversations with them, feeling like you, too, will make it to the other side.

Then there will be the people who simply do not "get it" and who may never "get it." It's not that they don't want to understand; they just can't. They simply haven't been through the battle that you are going through. Unfortunately, in their present form of not "getting it," they may very well inflict more wounds on your already wounded heart by telling you what God's will is for your life. You walk away from conversations with these individuals feeling like you're already limping along heart was just flattened by a semi-truck.

The reality is that no one, and I mean no one, can know what God's will is for our lives except for Him and how He chooses to reveal that to us. (I mean, really, most of the time, it's hard enough to figure out what God's will is for our own lives, much less trying to nail it down for anyone else's.) Although our hurting hearts cry out in desperation to be heard and understood, that desperation can cloud our already murky vision in the choices we make, the emotions that we too freely choose to share, and the God-given promises we reveal.

In your time of waiting, ask God to reveal to you whom it is safe to share the most tender parts of your heart. Ask God to connect you with those people who are walking the same path or who have walked the same path. And until He does, know that He is right there with you, promising,

> Never will I leave you;
> Never will I forsake you.[293]

And as the Author of every emotion we have ever had, are having, and will ever have, I can assure you, He "gets it."

Chapter 8

God's Promises if We are Willing to Wait

God's promises to those who wait upon Him are many and powerful. We are told in the Bible that:

- All things will work together for good.
- We will soar like wings with eagles.
- He will make beauty from our ashes.
- He will not waste the pain.
- He will give us strength to endure.
- He will bless us.

Specifically, Isaiah 30:18 says, "Yet the Lord longs to be gracious to you; therefore He will rise up to show you compassion. For the Lord is a God of justice. Blessed are all who wait for Him!"[294] Luke 1:45 encourages us, "Blessed is she who has believed that the Lord would fulfill His promises to her!"[295] And Isaiah 64:4 tells us, "Since ancient times no one has heard, no ear has perceived, no eye has seen any God besides you, who acts on behalf of those who wait for Him."[296] God longs to bless us abundantly when we are willing to wait for His best.

I want to repeat that statement because I think it is so crucial for us to understand. God longs to bless us abundantly when we are willing to wait for His best. He wants to give us good things when we are willing to wait for them. Perhaps that's because He knows just how hard it is to wait and how easy it would be to accept a substitute.

Other than these broad promises of Scripture, there are times in our lives where we believe that God has given us an individual promise. It is our special promise just to us and for us. It is something we felt in our spirit and is sometimes confirmed through dreams or visions or other people. Satan desperately wants us to doubt those promises. Sometimes, as I am sure Abraham did, we may doubt that God even made a promise to us. But deep down, we know that He did. How do we know? Because even when we may fear that perhaps God didn't promise something to us still, deep inside, we keep waiting. We keep expecting what we hope for to happen one day.

God's promises are guarantees, and although sometimes the night stretches into the morning, the morning will come. His delays are not denials. The promise will come for the "One who calls you is faithful, and He will do it."[297]

Thankfully, God provides us examples of His promises being fulfilled and, in many cases, fulfilled despite all human logic. Again, Abraham is a prime example. We are told, "after waiting patiently, Abraham received what was promised."[298]

> Abraham was tested for a very long time, but he was richly rewarded. The Lord tested him by delaying the fulfillment of His promise. Satan tested him through temptation, and people tested him through their jealousy, distrust, and opposition to him. Sarah, his own wife, tested him through her worrisome temperament. Yet he patiently endured, not questioning God's truthfulness and power or doubting God's faithfulness and love. Instead, Abraham submitted to God's divine sovereignty and infinite wisdom. And he was silent through many delays, willing to wait for the Lord's timing. Having patiently endured, he then obtained the fulfillment of the promise.[299]

God promised Abraham he would be the father of a great nation. But at seventy-five, Abraham had no children. After twenty-five years of waiting and God coming to Abraham in many ways and at different times to affirm the original promise, the promised son Isaac was born.

Why was Abraham able to hang on for those twenty-five long years despite those around him, including his wife, doubting God's promise? Because He knew that the One who had made the promise was faithful. Hebrews 10:23 tells us, "Let us hold unswervingly to the hope we profess, for He who promised is faithful."[300]

Perhaps Abraham was also able to hang on because he recognized two major things about God's promises. With all Abraham had seen in his time walking with the Lord, I believe he recognized that God's promises don't always follow natural or human logic. Sarah was far past normal, biological, child-bearing age. In fact, she had already hit menopause. But God isn't bound by the normal laws of nature, and therefore even time could not defeat His plan.

Abraham knew this, and he knew that nothing is impossible with God. Luke 1:37 says, "For no word from God will ever fail."[301] The things that are impossible with men are possible with God. No matter how great the obstacle, God is greater. Abraham set God free to be God. He didn't know how God would do it, but he knew that He would. We must stay convinced that what God has promised us, God is able to do. And in the meantime, we grow strong in our faith. We refuse to waiver in our unbelief. We consider Him faithful. We, too, set God free.

Perhaps Abraham also recognized that God's promises come in His time, not ours. Although Abraham may have loved to have a son in his younger years so he could run and play with the young child, God had a different timetable. Abraham wasn't privy to the why, but he did know the Who...and that was enough for him to patiently wait until the promise was fulfilled.

All Things Work Together for Good

In the midst of my deepest, darkest pain and my inability to wait one second longer, I cling to Romans 8:28, "And we know that in all things God works for the good of those who love Him, who have been called according to His purpose."[302] Paul does not tell us that "in most things," "in some things," "in really happy things," or "in the big things," God works. He tells us that "in all things God works."

159

Stop and think of the range of this promise for just a second. "In all things" means that from the tiniest of details in our lives to the biggest decisions that we are faced with, God is at work. Even more interesting, Paul uses the present tense of "works." Paul does not say "God worked" or "God will work," but rather "God works." This tells us that God's working is a continuous operation. So, the bottom line is that God works—in all things, big and little—and He is working all the time.

As we dig into the verse again, we find that "in all things God works for the good of those who love him." "For the good of those who love him" lifts my heavy heart. The verse doesn't just tell us that God is working behind the scenes, but that God is working for our good. "In a thousand trials, it is not just five hundred of them that work 'for the good' of the believer, but nine hundred and ninety-nine, plus one.

> Your Lord, who sees the end from the beginning,
> Has purposes for you of love untold.
> Then place your hand in His and follow fearless,
> Till you the riches of His grace behold.[303]

Sometimes we find it all impossible to fathom, but Jesus knew this and said, "You do not realize now what I am doing, but later you will understand."[304] You see, "[when] God desires to create more power in your life, He creates more friction. He uses this pressure to generate spiritual power. Receive the power and use it to rise above the painful experience that produced it. The pressures of temptations and trials and all the things that seem to be against us further our progress and strengthen our foundation."[305]

So through the pain of waiting, we must remind ourselves, "that in all things God works for the good of those who love Him, who have been called according to His purpose."[306] It isn't just a lovely verse to boost our spirits. It's a God-given promise to light our way until the difficult and heart-wrenching journey has ended.

We Will Soar with Wings like Eagles

Another one of God's promises while we wait is that we will soar with wings like eagles as we hope in the Lord. (We touched on this verse before, but it is worth exploring again from a different angle.) Isaiah 40:28-31 tells us:

> Do you not know?
> Have you not heard?
> The LORD is the everlasting God,
> the Creator of the ends of the earth.
> He will not grow tired or weary,
> and his understanding no one can fathom.
> He gives strength to the weary
> and increases the power of the weak.
> Even youths grow tired and weary,
> and young men stumble and fall;
> but those who hope in the LORD
> will renew their strength.
> They will soar on wings like eagles;
> they will run and not grow weary,
> they will walk and not be faint.[307]

This verse beautifully captures the idea that God cannot and does not grow weary or tired. He is the source of all energy and all strength. So, when we are feeling tired and weary and stumbling and falling along, we simply need to plug our hope back into the power source of the Lord. When we do so, we will renew our strength, we will soar on wings like eagles, we will run and not grow weary, and we will walk and not faint.

Now, there is a caveat here regarding soaring with wings like eagles. This does not mean during our trial that our hearts will suddenly be soaring with happiness. Quite the contrary, the trial we are in may be

161

taking us into a depth of despair that we had not previously imagined existed. However, our soaring has to do with soaring towards God. The storms of the trial, if we spread our spiritual wings, lift us up higher to the Lord because we become completely focused on Him and His will for our lives.

Why would God use the analogy of the eagle? It may be because of how eagles fly when they encounter storms. They literally let the currents of the storm push them higher and higher above the storm itself until they find calm skies. When we put our hope in the Lord and open our wings right in the face of our trials, those trials will push us into a higher, deeper, more intimate relationship with the Lord. And God will give us the strength to face down our fears, to bear the burden of waiting, to wrestle with our doubts, and to resist the temptation to turn and run from that which is so hard.

The heavy loads we bear as we wait can literally be the catalyst for amazing transformation in our lives if we continue to hope in the Lord.

> Our burden are our wings; on them
> We soar to higher realms of grace;
> Without them we must ever roam
> On plains of undeveloped faith,
> (For faith grows but by exercise
> In circumstances impossible.)
> The load we think will crush was sent to lift us up to God![308]

He Will Make Beauty from Ashes

God also promises us that He will make beauty from the ashes of our lives. In Isaiah 61:1-3, we are told:

> He has sent me to bind up the brokenhearted,
> to proclaim freedom for the captives

> and release from darkness for the prisoners,
> to proclaim the year of the LORD's favor
> and the day of vengeance of our God,
> to comfort all who mourn,
> and provide for those who grieve in Zion—
> to bestow on them a crown of beauty
> instead of ashes,
> the oil of joy
> instead of mourning,
> and a garment of praise
> instead of a spirit of despair.[309]

Comfort for those who mourn. Beauty instead of ashes. Joy instead of mourning. Praise instead of despair. I really like God's trade-in policy.

His trade-in policy includes those ashes in our lives that were of our own making. It includes those ashes that are remnants from our bad choices and bad decisions and even our greatest failures. The reality is that we are all going to have failures in our lives. In fact, at times, God permits failures in our lives because failures of a significant magnitude often bring with them the "greatest victories, the deepest lessons, and the most lasting changes."[310] God can take the failures and mistakes of our lives, rebuild our lives, and make them more beautiful than we could have imagined. He specializes in making beauty from ashes.

He Will Not Waste the Pain

Another beautiful promise we have as we wait on God is that He will not waste the pain. God is the great recycler. He lets no event, no situation, no tragedy in our lives go to waste. Whether it was our own poor decisions or actions, or someone else's decisions or hurtful actions, God will not let the pain of what we have been through or are going through go to waste. He recycles our hurt, pain, and tears into something with far greater purpose and greater meaning in our lives.

In fact, it is our painful experiences that God can use the most to prepare us to minister to others. Our greatest life messages and our most effective ministries will often come out of our deepest hurts. "If you really desire to be used by God, you must understand a powerful truth: The very experiences that you have resented or regretted most in life—the ones you've wanted to hide and forget—are the experiences God wants to use to help others. They are your ministry."[311]

"For God to use your painful experiences, you must be willing to share them."[312] "The things you're most embarrassed about, most ashamed of, and most reluctant to share are the very tools God can use most powerfully to heal others. You have to stop covering them up, and you must honestly admit your faults, failures, and fears."[313]

So, when we are in the deep, deep valley of pain during our waiting time, we have to remind ourselves that God will not waste the pain. As Jason Gray sings in his song "Nothing Is Wasted,"

[W]hat if every tear you cry, will seed the ground where joy will grow. And nothing is wasted. In the hands of our Redeemer, nothing is wasted. It's from the deepest wounds that beauty finds a place to bloom and you will see before the end that every broken piece is gathered in the heart of Jesus and what's lost will be found again. From the wreckage, from the darkness glory will shine.

He Will Give Us Strength to Endure

As we wait, God has promised to give us strength to endure. He didn't say our waiting would be easy, and He didn't say that the waiting time would be a few minutes, hours, or days. But He did promise us that He would be our source of strength when the going got tough, and we felt as if each step would undoubtedly be the one that brought us to our knees.

The Psalms are filled with verses that capture this idea of God being our strength and giving us strength, but there are three that appear to capture the essence of this idea the most concretely. Psalm 18:32 says, "It is God who arms me with strength and keeps my way secure."[314] Even in the tough time of waiting, He is arming us with strength and keeping our way safe.

Psalm 46:1 follows up by reminding us that "God is our refuge and strength, an ever-present help in trouble."[315] No matter how deep we believe our pool of trouble has become, He is there. And when our bodies and hearts begin to fail because of the toil our waiting has taken on us, Psalm 73:26 reminds us, "My flesh and my heart may fail, but God is the strength of my heart and my portion forever."[316]

Why does He promise to give us strength to keep going? "He knows how we are formed, He remembers that we are dust."[317] He remembers exactly what we were made of and how we were made—because He made us. And He will never ask us to take one step more than we are able to endure without His present arm being there to pick us up if we fall.

He Will Bless Us and Encourage Us

On top of the promises that God has already provided us, we know that there are special blessings for those who wait on Him, as waiting is one of the most difficult exhortations in all of Scripture. Isaiah 30:18 reminds us, "Yet the LORD longs to be gracious to you; therefore He will rise up to show you compassion. For the LORD is a God of justice. Blessed are all who wait for Him!"[318] And if we are willing to wait on God, Psalm 37:6 tells us that God longs to make our "righteous reward shine like the dawn" and our "vindication like the noonday sun."[319]

As we continue to wait for our righteous rewards, God is gracious enough to provide encouragement along the way...even ever so small.

It may be a song, a poem, or a kind word from a friend that just lifts our hearts when we start to get discouraged. Sometimes God even uses His spiritual highlighter to make sure we see the things He wants and needs us to see.

No matter how long we wait, we must "[r]est assured that if God waits longer than we desire, it is simply to make the blessings doubly precious."[320] And we can also rest assured that He will accomplish those things He has promised!

Chapter 9

God's Appointed Time

God has an appointed time for everything in our lives. Everything. Every situation, every promise, everything...has a God-appointed time. Yes, this also includes the end of our waiting. In fact, Habakkuk 2:3 tells us, "For the revelation awaits an appointed time; it speaks of the end and will not prove false. Though it linger, wait for it; it will certainly come and will not delay."[321]

As we wait for God's appointed time of our promised revelation, there are some myths that we need to strike from our hearts and some points of fact that we need to ponder. So, let's dive right into the myths. I believe that there are two myths that Satan bombards us with during our time of waiting. The first myth is that God has forgotten about us. I can just hear Satan whispering in my ear, "God has sadly forgotten about you. I mean, look at the time that has elapsed between when He gave you the promise and the godly desires began to well up in your heart, to today. It's been a long time, and He has so many incredibly important things going on that He just forgot your little issue."

These are nothing but lies. Our God, who loves us enough to know the very number of hairs on our heads and who catches each and every tear drop that falls from our eyes, has not forgotten about us. Deuteronomy 31:6 reminds us of this when it says, "Be strong and courageous...for the Lord your God goes with you; He will never leave you nor forsake you."[322] Although Satan would love us to believe differently, our God will never leave us, never forsake us, and never forget about us. He simply can't. He loves us too much.

The second myth we need to debunk is that our afflictions will never come to an end. Although in our present circumstances, it appears that our trial of waiting has us caught in an eternal spiral that will never end, it will end. Nahum 1:12 says, "Although I have afflicted you...I will afflict you no more."[323] There is a limit to our affliction. The Lord of the harvest is not in the business of threshing us for the rest of our earthly lives. The trials He allows to enter our lives have a season, and that season will come to an end.

When God has accomplished His purpose in the trial we find ourselves, and He lifts the affliction that has been plaguing us; night will turn into day, the clouds covering the sky will disappear, and our bone-deep sorrow will be transformed into joy that emanates from our very toes. As Psalm 30:5 exhorts us, "Weeping may stay for the night, but rejoicing comes in the morning."[324] "Even the fact that we face a trial proves there is something very precious to our Lord in us, or else He would not spend so much time and energy on us. Christ would not test us if He did not see the precious metal of faith mingled with the rock core of our nature, and it is to refine us into purity and beauty that He forces us through the fiery ordeal."[325]

Now that we have debunked two myths that Satan would love us to buy into, let's look at the truths about God's appointed time. As I have studied God's Word about His appointed time, I have found five truths that really stood out to me, and they are as follows:

- God's appointed time is impeccable.
- God's appointed time is not ours to command.
- God's appointed time is full of purpose.
- God's appointed time is unique to each one of us.
- God's appointed time is worth the wait.

So, let's un-package each one of these, starting with the first: God's appointed time is impeccable. As we study Scriptures, we see repeatedly that God's timing was impeccable. Whether it was the parting of the Red Sea, helping the Israelites overcome their adversaries in battle, or God-fearing men and women overcoming incredible odds, God's timing is always just perfect. We never find

Him to be early or too late...always right on time...and always in a way that gives Him the most glory.

Our second point to ponder is that God's appointed time is not ours to command. God always hears our prayers and the cries of our hearts, but He may not answer our prayers at the precise time we have appointed to be the perfect time. As I think back on my own life, I would say that my "perfect time" was never ever God's appointed time. In my desperate need to try to control my own situation, I still tried to lay out the best timeline for God. (I can only imagine how many times He has shaken His head and laughed at my inability to grasp the fact that my timelines are always a bit off. Okay, really off!)

> In the old days of flint, steel, and brimstone matches, people had to strike the match, again and again, perhaps even dozens of times, before they could get a spark to light their fire, and they were very thankful if they finally succeeded. Should we not exercise the same kind of perseverance and hope regarding heavenly things? When it comes to faith, we have more certainty of success than we could ever have had with flint and steel, for we have God's promises as a foundation.

> May we, therefore, never despair. God's time for mercy will come—in fact, it has already come if our time for believing has arrived. Ask in faith without wavering, but never cease to petition the King simply because He has delayed His reply. Strike the match again and make the sparks fly. Yet be sure to have your tinder ready, for you will get a fire before long. I do not believe there is such a thing in the history of God's eternal kingdom as a right prayer offered in the right spirit that remains forever unanswered.[326]

Our third point is that God's appointed time is full of purpose. Sometimes we have an inkling of what that purpose for our waiting may be, and sometimes we have absolutely no idea. But when the hard times come, and they will, we cannot allow ourselves to fall into despair and try to escape our trials prematurely. We must remind ourselves, as Ecclesiastes 3:1-8 tells us, there is a time for everything:

> There is a time for everything,
> and a season for every activity under the heavens:
> a time to be born and a time to die,
> a time to plant and a time to uproot,
> a time to kill and a time to heal,
> a time to tear down and a time to build,
> a time to weep and a time to laugh,
> a time to mourn and a time to dance,
> a time to scatter stones and a time to gather them,
> a time to embrace and a time to refrain from embracing,
> a time to search and a time to give up,
> a time to keep and a time to throw away,
> a time to tear and a time to mend,
> a time to be silent and a time to speak,
> a time to love and a time to hate,
> a time for war and a time for peace.[327]

There is a season for every activity under heaven, and each season has a prescribed God-given purpose in our lives. And we will see that "He has made everything beautiful in its time."[328]

The fourth point to ponder is that God's appointed time is unique to each one of us. There are times I do wish it was all prescribed, giving us at least a range in which we fall into for God's timing for our waiting to end. We don't get a range, and most times, we don't have any idea of what the timetable might look like.

God's timing is simply unique for each one of us in terms of the end of our waiting and what He is trying to accomplish in our lives. Sometimes God rescues us in the darkest of nights when we have absolutely nothing left and are about to dive off the cliff of despair. Sometimes God rescues us after we have already fallen off the cliff and are inches away from hitting ground zero. Other times He rescues us after we have stepped away from that cliff of sorrow and some healing has occurred.

When we look at biblical history, God saved the Israelites in their darkest night when the Egyptians had chased them right to the Red Sea and death was a certainty. On the other hand, Job was only rescued after healing had occurred, and he was even at the point of praying for forgiveness for the very friends that had so deeply hurt him. In each situation, God's timing was unique for His children, just as His timing is unique for each one of us.

The fifth and final point for us to ponder is that God's appointed time is worth the wait. As we pray daily, expecting an answer, it can be difficult to process that God's delays are not denials. In fact, God simply can't wait to bless us, but only when the blessings are ripe. We on the other hand, too frequently try to pluck our blessings from the tree when they are still a bit green.

God knows the perfect order and timing of the answers to our prayers and the giving of His blessings. He also knows, although we may have a tough time admitting it, waiting on Him may provide us even greater satisfaction than if our blessing came too quickly. So, take heart! The One we wait for will not disappoint us. He will not be late for the appointed time. And we will find that the waiting was more than worth it.

Speaking from personal experience, I know that to be true. A few years back, I tore my ACL for the second time at a kids' Christian sports camp while playing soccer with a group of campers. After having torn it once, I knew exactly what I had done and exactly what the road ahead was going to look like. It wasn't going to be pretty. Having your ACL reconstructed and having to work through the rehabilitation is one of the most difficult surgeries a competitive athlete can face. It gets as basic as having to teach yourself to bend your knee again, then to walk, and then to run again.

Not by choice but by necessity, I waited to have my second ACL reconstruction for two years. Between the inability to get in to see a surgeon and the starting of a new job, there simply wasn't a good time to begin the year-long process of getting back to 100 percent.

So, I waited and prayed, and prayed and waited. During that two years of waiting, God ended up working a miracle and healed my ACL that two doctors said was torn and confirmed by two different MRIs. In fact, I woke up in the surgical room to hear my doctor saying, "Well, I don't know what to say, but her ACL is fine." Waiting not only resulted in a blessing, but it also resulted in a miracle. A genuine, modern-day miracle.

When we look back through Scriptures, we find that Job's waiting on God, even when it was crushing his heart and soul, resulted in blessings beyond compare. As Job 42:12 tells us, "The Lord blessed the later part of Job's life more than the former part."[329] It wasn't easy, but I am sure when we get to heaven, Job will echo the thought that waiting on God's appointed time was well worth the wait.

With these five truths in mind, we must set aside Satan's lies and never run impulsively before the Lord. We must learn to wait for God's timing—the second, the minute, the hour that He has ordained. We must open our hearts and eyes to the miracles that may be waiting just around the corner. We must be willing to suffer through the waiting, always willing to wait for the "great." The great is coming, and Isaiah 30:18 encourages with this, "Yet the Lord longs to be gracious to you; therefore He will rise up to show you compassion. For the Lord is a God of justice. Blessed are all who wait for Him!"[330]

Chapter 10

Conclusion

We all will have periods of waiting in our lives, whether they are short-lived or long-lasting. The long-lasting periods of waiting carry with them an emotional burden, and in some cases, a burden so heavy it is difficult to make it through the day. What we are waiting on can vary from a job to healing for a painful health issue, to Mr. or Ms. Right coming into your life, or for the blessing to become parents. The bottom line is the hardest waiting time is when we are waiting for the deepest desires and longings of our hearts to be fulfilled.

You see, we often have the most wonderful ideas about when something in our lives should occur—down to the date and the time. Often, however, our ideas on timing are light years apart from God's plans. So, we must surrender to His timing, and when we do, He can do amazing things in us and for us. The hard part is reminding ourselves that God acts on behalf of those who wait for Him, and He wants the very, very best for us. In fact, the Bible tells us, "Since ancient times no one has heard, no ear has perceived, no eye has seen any God besides you, who acts on behalf of those who wait for Him."[331]

Waiting on the Lord means we look to Him in expectation and eagerly anticipate what He is about to do. It sounds so easy, right? I can look to the Lord in eager expectation, and yes, I am eagerly anticipating what He is about to do. And yet, when that waiting lasts day after day, week after week, month after month, year after year, it is one of the hardest things the Lord will ever ask us to do.

Compound that pain of waiting with the pain waiting for the deepest desires and longings of our hearts to be fulfilled. We know that God is the Giver of Dreams and the One who has placed desires deep inside each one of our hearts. He has given us gifts, skills, and talents that we dream about using in different ways. He gives us dreams about our future in terms of relationships and family.

Our God-given desires are bolstered by God's Promises. Psalm 37:4 says, "Take delight in the Lord, and he will give you the desires of your heart."[332] This is God's precious Promise to us...that when we delight ourselves in Him, He will give us the very desires of our heart.

As we wait for the desires of our hearts, the reality is that waiting is a choice. Now mind you, it isn't an easy choice, but it is a choice, and it is our choice to make. What I have found during my own period of waiting was that it wasn't a choice I made once, but rather a choice that I had to make over and over and over again, minute by minute, hour by hour.

I wish I could tell you that when we make the choice to wait, the waiting will be easy. But it's not. There are moments of darkness and despair that are all-encompassing. But the light will shine through again. There are moments of pain and suffering that seem like they will never end. But they will. There are times when it seems that the trial of your waiting will continue forever. But it won't. I promise. There are times that the weariness of waiting will seem to set in deep into your bones until you feel that taking one more step is beyond your ability. But that's when God's sustaining grace will be there to give us the strength to fight on one more day.

As hard as the waiting is, God has a purpose behind everything that we encounter in our lives. There is always an answer to the "why" question, even the "why-do-we-have-to-wait" question. Although simplistic, we often must wait for four reasons:

1. God is arranging the circumstances.
2. God is refining us like gold.
3. God is preparing us for what He has in store for us.
4. God is bringing us into true intimacy with Himself.

These reasons don't necessarily make the waiting easier, but at least they help us understand why we might be in this waiting period.

Sometimes God also has to take a little of Egypt out of us, so we stop looking backward at what we have foregone and start looking forward to the future God has in store for us.

But waiting on God, no matter how good the reasons are, is no task for the faint of heart. It requires so much of us, and often more than we believe we have to make it day to day. Waiting on God requires us to have faith, patience, humility, courage, and perseverance. It requires each of these in abundant supply.

These character traits are bolstered by how we choose to wait. We can wait with exasperation, stomping our feet every day until God brings the waiting to an end, or we can wait in a way that reveals the extent to which we trust the One we are ultimately waiting for—God. When we wait in a manner of total trust, we find ourselves clinging to God, calling on His name, depending on Him, being honest with Him, and fixing our eyes on Him. We also find that we can continue to hope expectantly as we let God lead, love Him, praise Him, pray to Him, seek Him, serve Him, and surrender to Him.

We can wait in this manner of total trust because we know that God delivers on His promises. As we look back through Scripture, we find that God made good on every single one of His many promises. And His promises to those who wait upon Him are many and powerful. We are told in the Bible that:

1. All things will work together for good
2. We will soar like wings with eagles
3. He will make beauty from our ashes
4. He will not waste the pain
5. He will give us strength to endure
6. He will bless us.

We just aren't told when these promises will come to fruition.

So, we faithfully wait, knowing that God has an appointed time for everything in our lives. Everything. Every situation, every promise...has a God-appointed time. In fact, Habakkuk 2:3 tells us,

"For the revelation awaits an appointed time; it speaks of the end and will not prove false. Though it linger, wait for it; it will certainly come and will not delay."[333]

As we have studied God's Word about His appointed time together, we have found five truths that really stood out:

1. God's appointed time is impeccable.
2. God's appointed time is not ours to command.
3. God's appointed time is full of purpose.
4. God's appointed time is unique to each one of us.
5. God's appointed time is worth the wait.

Our trial of waiting will come to an end. The fire will have been hotter at times than we believed we could survive, and the pain unbearable. We can trust that God has His hand on the thermostat, and He knows just when the firing process has achieved all it was intended to achieve. "Great faith must first endure great trials. God's greatest gifts come through great pain."[334] In the meantime, we can climb closer to God on that path of pain, knowing that God walks with us in the midst of our trials and it's in the valleys that we grow.

My Own Waiting Period

During my own time of waiting, I have felt like Abraham with Isaac as I was called to obediently lay down something very precious to me—not knowing anything about what my future would hold. I have felt like Joseph being given dreams so real about my future and yet feeling like I couldn't be farther from those dreams being achieved. I have felt like David—going through such lows and then peaks of triumph. I have felt like Job—with the hurt and emotions literally devastating me to the point that I asked the Lord to end the pain or end me. I have felt like Joshua—shouting at the walls of Satan's lies to come crashing down. And yes, I have even felt like Noah—building the ark God called him to build, as I bought the ark God called me to buy in the form of a dresser.

This waiting gave me time for more reflection and soul searching than I had ever done previously in my life. I asked God about a million questions during this time, and I asked myself a couple hundred. One of the questions I had to ask myself was, "Do I want a good story?" Because wonderful stories come from situations and circumstances where it simply doesn't look like God will come through, and then He does in a way that is nothing short of miraculous.

I mean, honestly, who of us would be able to recall the story of the Israelites crossing the Red Sea even remotely if they had just taken a boat across, walked over a bridge, or swam it? I would venture to say none of us. So, God did something spectacular when the Israelites had their backs up against the wall (or the Red Sea in this case), and they had nowhere else to go and no one else to go to. The result is that their story is one that we simply can't forget.

So, "do I want a good story?" I do. I want a good story. But even more so, I want a miraculous story. Not only so that I can tell of God's miraculous power, but so that I will never, ever forget what He has brought me through and just how great is His power. I know me, and I know that if He doesn't absolutely blow my mind, I have the tendency to forget just how amazing He is and what awesome things He has brought to pass in my own life.

Not only will I feel blessed that I have a great story to tell, but I also believe that God has transformed me and will continue to transform me in a number of ways. I was transformed from a woman who would do my devotions on an inconsistent basis into one who didn't miss a morning devotional in over a year and a half. I was transformed from a woman who prayed on occasion—most notably in those "Jesus Emergency" moments—into one who became a prayer warrior for the things that God placed upon my heart. And I was transformed from a woman who was laser-focused on her "to-do" list into one who was laser-focused on carving out time for relationships. (Now, don't get me wrong, those "to-do" lists still get done. They just don't get done at the expense of spending time with those I love.)

Encouragement for You

God has an appointed time for everything. Our appointed time, if we are honest, is always right now. But right now, it isn't always what is best for us for a host of different reasons. Proverbs 16:9 reminds us, "In their hearts humans plan their course, but the LORD establishes their steps."[335]

If we want God's richest blessings in our lives, we need to wait not only on His will but also on His timing. That will allow His perfect plan for our lives to reveal itself in His perfect timing. Then we will see that God has better ways of getting us where we need to be when we need to be there and how we need to get there than we could ever plan for ourselves.

Sometimes we need a reminder that if God is asking us to wait on Him, it's not because He's forgotten us. It's because He was putting everything in place so He could do the unimaginable. Ephesians 3:20 encourages us by saying, "Now to Him who is able to do immeasurably more than all we ask or imagine, according to His power that is at work within us."[336] So, if God tells you to sit tight, *sit tight!* Those that reap the greatest blessings are those who were willing to sit tight.

Even if your situation looks impossible, we deal with a God who specializes in the impossible and miraculous. It is never too late for Him to do the impossible. We have a God who delights in impossibilities and who asks, "Is anything too hard for Me?"[337]

When it seems like the impossible is anything but probable, it is most often the time we need to sit in stillness before the God of the Universe. Although it may seem like being still is doing nothing, that couldn't be farther from the truth. As Beth Moore says, "Trusting in a God you cannot see is a long shot from nothing. Holding your tongue is a long shot from nothing. Being patient is a long shot from nothing. Counting it all, joy is a long shot from nothing. Submitting is a long shot from nothing. Resting in Christ is a long shot from nothing. Praying is a long shot from nothing."

> Someday we will understand that God has a reason for every "wait" He gives us through the course of our lives. When God's people are worried and concerned that their prayers are not being answered, how often we have seen Him working to answer them in a greater way! When has God ever taken anything from a person without restoring it many times over? [I]t is true that God never touches the heart with a trial without intending to bestow a greater gift or compassionate blessing.[338]

So, when you get down as your waiting drags on, it is vital to understand that waiting is not an interruption of God's plan...it is His plan. You see, there is a bridge between doing the will of God in terms of your waiting as He has directed and receiving His promise... and that bridge is endurance. Like a runner running a race, you can't lead the pack of other runners for five miles and then quit with two miles to go and expect to claim the prize. You have to have endurance to keep going until you have crossed the finish line.

Every athlete worth their salt has a story about how they had to push through incredible pain, circumstances, or issues at one time or another to claim the prize they had set their eyes on. The beauty of your situation is that some random person or race official was not the one who charted out your current race course. God did, and He knew exactly how long to make the course so it would make you but not break you.

So have faith, and know that there are three ways—like Abraham—you can let your waiting, and this testing strengthen your faith: 1. Recognize that waiting is an opportunity to know God better through spending time in His Word—thus developing a deeper sense of His character, wisdom, power, and plan. 2. Recognize that waiting is an opportunity to know yourself better. As you wait, your heart is revealed, and you have the amazing opportunity to become a student of your own heart. 3. Recognize that waiting is an opportunity to know others better.

A Praise and A Prayer

I want to end with Psalm 103, as I praise God for all that He has done in my life over tall the waiting I have faced throughout my life. I want to praise Him for all that He has taught me throughout my waiting period...things I would never have learned about Him, about myself, and about those I hold dear. And I want to praise Him for finally bringing this period of waiting in my life to an end. I know there will inevitably be others, but on this one we can firmly plant the victory flag.

I also want to thank Him on your behalf for all that He will do in and through you. There will be things occurring during your own waiting period—in yourself and in your circumstances—that you may never fully grasp until you are on the other side of your waiting period or on the other side of eternity. But they are occurring, and they are having an eternal impact.

Praise God that He is the model of patiently waiting and that He doesn't check His watch like we check ours!

Epilogue

Our God, the Keeper of Time, loves us so much that He knows the exact instant in which our waiting will come to an end. And we will be blessed beyond our imagination for patiently waiting for his best.

I can assure you, in every instance where I truly surrendered and obediently waited, whether it was an hour or a day or twelve years, it was worth every second of time and every tear shed.

The waiting times in my life have been difficult beyond description, but they have transformed me into the woman I am today. And they served as God's chiseling tool to ensure I was ready for the blessings He was about to bestow on me.

Lord Jesus, thank You for Your love for each one of us and knowing that the periods of waiting You introduce into our lives are a gift. And the ultimate gift is how the waiting periods bring us into a relationship with You, unlike anything we have ever known.

About the Author

Rachel Williams holds a PhD in Organization and Management with a specialization in Leadership from Capella University, whose dissertation was focused on Emotional Intelligence and its correlation to Leadership style. She also holds two degrees from Virginia Tech—an MBA and a BA with a double major in Political Science and Philosophy and double minors in English and Sociology.

She is an Engineering/Operations Executive at a Fortune-Fifty company and loves to put her educational learnings into practice with those employees she has the honor of leading and serving.

In her spare time, Rachel is an avid adventure seeker who loves skiing, hiking, biking, swimming, white water rafting, and traveling to beautiful places with her boyfriend, Sam. You will often find her six-year-old Samoyed pup, Kallie, and Sam's eight-year-old pup, Cheyenne, along with members of her very tight-knit family and dear friends joining in the fun. Rachel is also an endurance athlete who finished her first Ironman in Madison, Wisconsin, in 2018 and is training for other endurance events.

Rachel is a native of Northern Virginia but loves calling Castle Pines, Colorado, her home now!

Notes

[1] Warren, Rick. The Purpose Driven Life. Grand Rapids, MI: Zondervan, 2002, p 308.

[2] Google.com

[3] NIV Psalm 130:5-6

[4] NIV Isaiah 64:4

[5] Cowman, L.B. *Streams in the Desert*. Grand Rapids, MI: Zondervan, 1997.

[6] NIV Psalm 37:4

[7] NIV Psalm 145:19

[8] NIV Genesis 12:1-2

[9] NIV Genesis 15:4

[10] NIV Genesis 15:5

[11] NIV Genesis 17:15

[12] NIV Genesis 17:19

[13] NIV Genesis 18:10

[14] NIV John 3:16

[15] NIV Romans 3:23

[16] NIV Romans 6:23

[17] NIV Romans 5:8

[18] KJV Revelation 3:20

[19] NKJV Ephesians 2:8-9

[20] NKJV John 10:10

[21] NIV Isaiah 50:10

[22] Knapp, Roger. 1997. *Life Struggles*. Retrieved from https://www.rogerknapp.com/inspire/struggle.htm.

[23] New American Standard Isaiah 45:3

[24] Cowman, L.B. *Streams in the Desert*. Grand Rapids, MI: Zondervan, 1997, p 136.

[25] Cowman, L.B. *Streams in the Desert*. Grand Rapids, MI: Zondervan, 1997, p 138.

[26] NIV Exodus 14:21

[27] Cowman, L.B. *Streams in the Desert*. Grand Rapids, MI: Zondervan, 1997, p 338.

[28] Walk by Faith Perpetual Calendar. DaySpring.

[29] NIV Galatians 6:9

[30] Cowman, L.B. *Streams in the Desert*. Grand Rapids, MI: Zondervan, 1997, p 463.

[31] NIV Psalm 69:1-3

[32] NIV Psalm 88:1-3

[33] NIV Job 30:26-27

[34] NIV Psalm 71:20

[35] NAS Psalm 27:13

[36] NIV Habakkuk 2:3

[37] NIV Joshua 1:6
[38] NIV Psalm 46:10
[39] NIV Psalm 34:18
[40] NIV Psalm 147:3
[41] NIV John 16:20-24
[42] Cowman, L.B. *Streams in the Desert*. Grand Rapids, MI: Zondervan, 1997, p 356.
[43] NIV 2 Corinthians 4:17
[44] Arthur et al. *Walking with God in the Quiet Places*. Eugene, Oregon: Harvest House Publishers, 2009, pg. 39
[45] NIV Psalm 30:5
[46] https://www.freedictionary.com
[47] NIV Job 2:9
[48] NIV Job 3:1-26
[49] NLT Psalm 56:8
[50] NIV Romans 8:32
[51] Cowman, L.B. *Streams in the Desert*. Grand Rapids, MI: Zondervan, 1997, p 312.
[52] Cowman, L.B. *Streams in the Desert*. Grand Rapids, MI: Zondervan, 1997, p 375.
[53] Cowman, L.B. *Streams in the Desert*. Grand Rapids, MI: Zondervan, 1997, p 40.
[54] NIV Philippians 3:10
[55] NIV Romans 8:29
[56] Cowman, L.B. *Streams in the Desert*. Grand Rapids, MI: Zondervan, 1997, p 121.
[57] NIV 1 Peter 4:12-13
[58] NIV Isaiah 52:14
[59] NIV Matthew 26:38
[60] NIV Matthew 26:39
[61] NIV Matthew 26:42
[62] NIV Matthew 26:43
[63] NIV Luke 22:44
[64] NIV 2 Corinthians 5:21
[65] NIV Matthew 27:46
[66] NIV Hebrews 2:10
[67] NIV Psalm 126:5
[68] NIV Psalm 84:11
[69] NIV Job 42:12-17
[70] NIV Psalm 138:7a
[71] NIV 2 Corinthians 4:7
[72] NIV 1 Peter 1:6-7
[73] Cowman, L.B. *Streams in the Desert*. Grand Rapids, MI: Zondervan, 1997, p 335.
[74] Wiersbe, Warren. *Be Mature*. Colorado Springs, CO: David C. Cook, 1978.

[75] NIV James 1:2

[76] Wiersbe, Warren. *Be Mature.* Colorado Springs, CO: David C. Cook, 1978.

[77] Wiersbe, Warren. *Be Mature.* Colorado Springs, CO: David C. Cook, 1978.

[78] NIV James 1:3-4

[79] NIV Romans 5:3-4

[80] Wiersbe, Warren. *Be Mature.* Colorado Springs, CO: David C. Cook, 1978.

[81] Wiersbe, Warren. *Be Mature.* Colorado Springs, CO: David C. Cook, 1978.

[82] Wiersbe, Warren. *Be Mature.* Colorado Springs, CO: David C. Cook, 1978.

[83] NIV Rom. 8:29

[84] Wiersbe, Warren. *Be Mature.* Colorado Springs, CO: David C. Cook, 1978.

[85] Wiersbe, Warren. *Be Mature.* Colorado Springs, CO: David C. Cook, 1978.

[86] NIV James 1:5-8

[87] NIV 2 Corinthians 4:16-18

[88] Cowman, L.B. *Streams in the Desert.* Grand Rapids, MI: Zondervan, 1997, p 140.

[89] NIV James 1:12

[90] Cowman, L.B. *Streams in the Desert.* Grand Rapids, MI: Zondervan, 1997, p 429

[91] Cowman, L.B. *Streams in the Desert.* Grand Rapids, MI: Zondervan, 1997, p 587.

[92] NIV Romans 8:37

[93] Cowman, L.B. *Streams in the Desert.* Grand Rapids, MI: Zondervan, 1997, p 587.

[94] NIV Nahum 1:12

[95] NIV Psalm 30:5

[96] Cowman, L.B. *Streams in the Desert.* Grand Rapids, MI: Zondervan, 1997, p 218.

[97] NIV Psalm 119:28

[98] NIV Psalm 69:3

[99] NIV Psalm 119:82

[100] Lewis. C.S. *Screwtape Letters.* New York, NY: Harper Collins, 1942, p 173.

[101] NIV Hebrews 4:16

[102] NIV 2 Corinthians 12:9

[103] NIV James 1:2-4

[104] NIV Galatians 6:9

[105] Cowman, L.B. *Streams in the Desert.* Grand Rapids, MI: Zondervan, 1997, p 294.

[106] NIV 1 Peter 1:6-8

[107] NIV Malachi 3:3

[108] http://www.gold-traders.co.uk/gold-information/how-to-refine-gold.asp

[109] http://www.google.com/#gs_rn=19&gs_ri=psy-ab&cp=18&gs_
id=23&xhr=t&q=meaning+of+crucible&es_nrs=true&p-
f=p&output=search&sclient=psy-ab&oq=meaning+of+%22cru-
cib&gs_l=&pbx=1&bav=on.2,or.r_qf.&bvm=bv.48705608,d.
dmg&fp=394031f0a24a0cea&biw=1440&bih=734

[110] NIV Job 23:10

[111] Author Unknown

[112] Cowman, L.B. *Streams in the Desert*. Grand Rapids, MI: Zondervan, 1997, p 428.

[113] Warren, Rick. *The Purpose Driven Life*. Grand Rapids, MI: Zondervan, 2002, p 220.

[114] Cowman, L.B. *Streams in the Desert*. Grand Rapids, MI: Zondervan, 1997, p 279.

[115] Cowman, L.B. *Streams in the Desert*. Grand Rapids, MI: Zondervan, 1997, p 415.

[116] Cowman, L.B. *Streams in the Desert*. Grand Rapids, MI: Zondervan, 1997, p 428.

[117] NIV Numbers 13:27-28

[118] NIV Numbers 13:31

[119] NIV Numbers 14:2-4

[120] NIV Numbers 14:11-12

[121] NIV Numbers 14:34-35

[122] NIV Jeremiah 29:11

[123] NIV Ephesians 3:20

[124] NIV James 5:7

[125] Cowman, L.B. *Streams in the Desert*. Grand Rapids, MI: Zondervan, 1997, p 283.

[126] Author Unknown

[127] Merriam-Webster. com/dictionary

[128] NIV Hebrews 11:1

[129] Cowman, L.B. *Streams in the Desert*. Grand Rapids, MI: Zondervan, 1997, p 280.

[130] Cowman, L.B. *Streams in the Desert*. Grand Rapids, MI: Zondervan, 1997, p 281.

[131] NIV Romans 4:18

[132] NIV Genesis 26:4

[133] NIV Romans 4:20-21

[134] NIV Psalm 139:13

[135] NIV Mark 9:23

[136] NIV Mark 11:24

[137] Cowman, L.B. *Streams in the Desert*. Grand Rapids, MI: Zondervan, 1997, p 79.

[138] Cowman, L.B. *Streams in the Desert*. Grand Rapids, MI: Zondervan, 1997, p 190.

[139] Cowman, L.B. *Streams in the Desert*. Grand Rapids, MI: Zondervan, 1997, p 192.

[140] Cowman, L.B. *Streams in the Desert*. Grand Rapids, MI: Zondervan, 1997, p 156.

[141] NIV Psalm 105:5

[142] NIV Psalm 107:27

[143] Cowman, L.B. *Streams in the Desert*. Grand Rapids, MI: Zondervan, 1997, p 423.

[144] NIV Ephesians 3:20

[145] Cowman, L.B. *Streams in the Desert*. Grand Rapids, MI: Zondervan, 1997, p 278.

[146] Cowman, L.B. *Streams in the Desert*. Grand Rapids, MI: Zondervan, 1997, p 269.

[147] NIV Acts 27:25

[148] Cowman, L.B. *Streams in the Desert*. Grand Rapids, MI: Zondervan, 1997, p 19.

[149] Cowman, L.B. *Streams in the Desert*. Grand Rapids, MI: Zondervan, 1997, p 268.

[150] Cowman, L.B. *Streams in the Desert*. Grand Rapids, MI: Zondervan, 1997, p 274.

[151] Merriam-Webster. com/dictionary

[152] Merriam-Webster. com/dictionary

[153] Barclay, William. New Testament Words, pp. 143-144

[154] KJV Hebrews 12:1

[155] Cowman, L.B. *Streams in the Desert*. Grand Rapids, MI: Zondervan, 1997, p 408-409.

[156] NIV Psalm 37:7-9

[157] NIV Psalm 46:10

[158] Cowman, L.B. *Streams in the Desert*. Grand Rapids, MI: Zondervan, 1997, p 408.

[159] Cowman, L.B. *Streams in the Desert*. Grand Rapids, MI: Zondervan, 1997, p 408.

[160] Cowman, L.B. *Streams in the Desert*. Grand Rapids, MI: Zondervan, 1997, p 153-154.

[161] NIV Exodus 14:14

[162] Cowman, L.B. *Streams in the Desert*. Grand Rapids, MI: Zondervan, 1997, p 145.

[163] Cowman, L.B. *Streams in the Desert*. Grand Rapids, MI: Zondervan, 1997, p 355.

[164] NIV Philippians 4:7

[165] NIV Isaiah 30:15

[166] NIV Psalm 119:165

[167] NIV 1 Kings 19:12

[168] Cowman, L.B. *Streams in the Desert*. Grand Rapids, MI: Zondervan, 1997, p 438.

[169] Wikipedia.com

[170] Merriam-Webster. com/dictionary

[171] NIV Deuteronomy 8:6

[172] NIV Deuteronomy 10:12

[173] NIV 1 Kings 11:38

[174] NIV Psalm 128:1

[175] NIV Jeremiah 7:23

[176] NIV Galatians 4:4

[177] NIV John 10:10

[178] Cowman, L.B. *Streams in the Desert*. Grand Rapids, MI: Zondervan, 1997, p 274.

[179] NIV Hebrews 6:15

[180] Cowman, L.B. *Streams in the Desert*. Grand Rapids, MI: Zondervan, 1997, p 275.

[181] Author unknown

[182] Merriam-Webster. com/dictionary

[183] NIV Genesis 7:5

[184] Dictionary. com

[185] NIV Joshua 1:9

[186] NIV Isaiah 41:10
[187] NIV Isaiah 41:13
[188] NIV Hebrews 3:5-6
[189] NIV Isaiah 43:1b-2
[190] NIV Psalm 34:4
[191] NIV Exodus 14:13
[192] Merriam-Webster. com/dictionary
[193] Dictionary. com
[194] My Utmost for His Highest
[195] NIV James 1:2-4
[196] NIV Romans 5:3-4
[197] NIV Hebrews 10:35-36
[198] NIV James 1:12
[199] NIV Galatians 6:9
[200] NIV James 5:11
[201] NIV Luke 18:1-6
[202] NIV Hebrews 12:1-4
[203] Matt Redman song: "You Never Let Go"
[204] Author Unknown
[205] Author Unknown
[206] NIV Hebrews 11:1
[207] NIV Genesis 32:26
[208] NIV Joel 2:32
[209] NIV 1 Samuel 13:14; Acts 13:22
[210] NIV Psalm 13:1-2
[211] NIV Psalm 13:5-6
[212] NIV Matthew 14:28
[213] NIV Romans 8:25
[214] NIV Proverbs 4:25
[215] NIV Psalm 123:1
[216] NIV Psalm 141:8
[217] NIV Hebrews 12:2
[218] NIV Philippians 3:12-14
[219] www. thefreedictionary. com
[220] NIV Ephesians 1:18-20
[221] NIV Psalm 39:7
[222] NIV Psalm 33:22
[223] NIV Psalm 42:11
[224] NIV Psalm 119:114

[225] NIV Psalm 130: 5
[226] NIV Lamentations 3:22
[227] NIV Romans 12:12
[228] NIV Hebrews 6:11-12
[229] NIV Romans 8:25
[230] NIV Isaiah 40:30-31
[231] NIV Psalm 62:5
[232] NIV 2 Thessalonians 2:16-17
[233] NIV Romans 15:13
[234] NIV Jeremiah 29:11
[235] NIV Proverbs 23:18
[236] NIV Hebrews 10:23
[237] NIV Lamentations 3:25
[238] NIV 1 Timothy 6:17
[239] NIV Romans 5:3-5
[240] Cowman, L.B. *Streams in the Desert.* Grand Rapids, MI: Zondervan, 1997, p 198.
[241] NIV Psalm 119:105
[242] NIV Psalm 126:3
[243] NIV Psalm 126:3
[244] NIV Psalm 134:1-2
[245] Cowman, L.B. *Streams in the Desert.* Grand Rapids, MI: Zondervan, 1997, p 460.
[246] NIV Psalm 103:2-13
[247] NIV Exodus 14:10-12
[248] NIV Isaiah 64:4
[249] NIV Mark 11:24
[250] NIV John 14:13
[251] NIV John 16:23
[252] Cowman, L.B. *Streams in the Desert.* Grand Rapids, MI: Zondervan, 1997, p 200.
[253] NIV John 15:7
[254] NIV 1 John 5:14-15
[255] NIV Genesis 24:14
[256] NIV Genesis 24:15
[257] NIV Romans 8:26-27
[258] Cowman, L.B. *Streams in the Desert.* Grand Rapids, MI: Zondervan, 1997, p 410-411.
[259] NIV Matthew 7:7
[260] NIV Luke 18:1
[261] NAS 1 Thessalonians 5:17
[262] Cowman, L.B. *Streams in the Desert.* Grand Rapids, MI: Zondervan, 1997, p 160.

[263] NIV Mark 10:27
[264] NIV Philippians 4:6-7
[265] NIV 1 Chronicles 16:11
[266] NIV 1 Chronicles 22:19
[267] NIV Psalm 63:1
[268] NIV Deuteronomy 4:29
[269] NIV Jeremiah 29:13
[270] NIV Proverbs 8:17
[271] NIV Hebrews 11:6
[272] NIV Lamentations 3:25
[273] NIV Psalm 9:10
[274] NIV Isaiah 30:20-21
[275] NIV 1 John 4:18
[276] NAS John 10:10
[277] NIV Job 22:21
[278] NIV Luke 9:24
[279] Cowman, L.B. *Streams in the Desert.* Grand Rapids, MI: Zondervan, 1997, p 258.
[280] Cowman, L.B. *Streams in the Desert.* Grand Rapids, MI: Zondervan, 1997, p 258.
[281] NIV Psalm 56:3
[282] NIV Psalm 52:8-9
[283] NIV Psalm 62:8
[284] NIV Psalm 4:5
[285] NIV Psalm 37:3
[286] NIV Psalm 9:10
[287] NIV Psalm 28:7
[288] NIV Psalm 37:4-6
[289] NIV Isaiah 26:3
[290] NIV Jeremiah 17:7
[291] NIV Proverbs 3:5-6
[292] NIV Romans 10:11
[293] NIV Hebrews 13:5
[294] NIV Isaiah 30:18
[295] NIV Luke 1:45
[296] NIV Isaiah 64:4
[297] NIV Thessalonians 5:24
[298] NIV Hebrews 6:15
[299] Cowman, L.B. *Streams in the Desert.* Grand Rapids, MI: Zondervan, 1997, p 346.
[300] NIV Hebrews 10:23
[301] NIV Luke 1:37

[302] NIV Romans 8:28

[303] Cowman, L.B. *Streams in the Desert*. Grand Rapids, MI: Zondervan, 1997, p 228.

[304] NIV John 13:7

[305] Cowman, L.B. *Streams in the Desert*. Grand Rapids, MI: Zondervan, 1997, p 147.

[306] NIV Romans 8:28

[307] NIV Isaiah 40:28-31

[308] Cowman, L.B. *Streams in the Desert*. Grand Rapids, MI: Zondervan, 1997, p 106.

[309] NIV Isaiah 61:3

[310] Carole Mayhall

[311] Warren, Rick. *The Purpose Driven Life*. Grand Rapids, MI: Zondervan, 2002, p 245.

[312] Warren, Rick. *The Purpose Driven Life*. Grand Rapids, MI: Zondervan, 2002, p 246.

[313] Warren, Rick. *The Purpose Driven Life*. Grand Rapids, MI: Zondervan, 2002, p 246.

[314] NIV Psalm 18:32

[315] NIV Psalm 46:1

[316] NIV Psalm 73:26

[317] NIV Psalm 103:14

[318] NIV Isaiah 30:18

[319] NIV Psalm 37:6

[320] Reference unknown

[321] NIV Habakkuk 2:3

[322] NIV Deuteronomy 31:6

[323] NIV Nahum 1:12

[324] NIV Psalm 30:5

[325] Cowman, L.B. *Streams in the Desert*. Grand Rapids, MI: Zondervan, 1997, p 77.

[326] Cowman, L.B. *Streams in the Desert*. Grand Rapids, MI: Zondervan, 1997, p 430.

[327] NIV Ecclesiastes 3:1-8

[328] NIV Ecclesiastes 3:11

[329] NIV Job 42:12

[330] NIV Isaiah 30:18

[331] NIV Isaiah 64:4

[332] NIV Psalm 37:4

[333] NIV Habakkuk 2:3

[334] Cowman, L.B. *Streams in the Desert*. Grand Rapids, MI: Zondervan, 1997, p 218.

[335] NIV Proverbs 16:9

[336] NIV Ephesians 3:20

[337] NIV Jeremiah 32:27

[338] Cowman, L.B. *Streams in the Desert*. Grand Rapids, MI: Zondervan, 1997, p 399.

CPSIA information can be obtained
at www.ICGtesting.com
Printed in the USA
BVHW040237140721
611841BV00013B/1149

9 781637 692882